Temple University

Intellectual Heritage
51

Fourth Edition

Key readings

The Ancient World

Religious Traditions

The Renaissance

Edited by

Marc Stier, Associate
Director, Intellectual
Heritage Program

Grant Ward, Associate
Director, Intellectual
Heritage Program

Daniel P. Tompkins,
Associate Professor of
Greek, Hebrew & Roman
Classics and Director,
Intellectual Heritage
Program

Istvan Varkonyi, Associate
Professor of German and
Associate Director,
Intellectual Heritage
Program

Jessie Braun Iwata,
Associate Director,
Intellectual Heritage
Program

 Temple University Press / Philadelphia

Temple University Press
1601 North Broad Street
Philadelphia PA 19122
www.temple.edu/tempress

Acknowledgments

Grateful acknowledgment is made to the following sources for permission to reprint material copyrighted or controlled by them:

Maps on page 26 reprinted from *Heritage of World Civilizations, Volume 1 to 1650,* 4th Edition, by Craig, Albert M.; Graham, William A.; Kagan, Donald; Ozment, Steven; Turner, Frank M.; copyright © 1997 by permission of Pearson Education, Inc., Upper Saddle River, NJ.

"Saint Augustine, *Confessions,* Book VII," reprinted from *Confessions* by Saint Augustine, translated by R.S. Pine-Coffin (Penguin Classics, 1961). Copyright © R.S. Pine-Coffin, 1961.

ISBN 1-59213-099-2

2 4 6 8 9 7 5 3 1

Contents

Preface

Key Readings I and *II* are the official collections of readings for Temple University's Intellectual Heritage Program as of the fall semester, 2001. The editors compiled these readings with specific goals in mind. They sought faculty consensus in developing readings that would be used by a large number of instructors and that students could buy at reasonable prices. Finally, they included a document that students must have access to, the Temple University Policy on Academic Dishonesty passed by the Faculty Senate. The editors also have included Professor Robin Mitchell-Boyask's introduction to his translations of Sappho in the Intellectual Heritage 51 reader. This exception seemed a worthwhile accompaniment to a translation done specifically for the program by a Temple faculty member.

Faculty commentary on these readings can now be found on the Intellectual Heritage Program website:

http://courses.temple.edu/ih

The existence of this rich and handy supportive material means that the current volume can be dedicated to the readings themselves, along with timelines and maps.

The editors express their gratitude to the large number of Temple University faculty who offered suggestions about the readings, to the staff of Temple University Press, and to the Intellectual Heritage Program Office Manager, Ms. Linda Tribune, for her unfailing good will and steady assistance throughout this process.

Introduction, translation, and notes by Robin Mitchell-Boyask, Department of Greek, Roman and Hebrew Classics

The Songs of Sappho

Introduction to Reading Sappho

When most people meet Sappho's songs for the first time, they are intrigued by the concept of a female poet in ancient Greece and want to know more about her, but ancient biographies are notoriously unreliable, and many myths have attached themselves to Sappho in particular because of the content of her poems. Thus, it is best to keep biography to a bare minimum. Sappho was likely born late in the 7th century B.C.E. on Lesbos, an island just off the coast of modern Turkey and quite close to Troy. This part of the Mediterranean was especially fertile culturally, as early science was born there and it also may have been the home of Homer. She probably endured exile to Sicily because of political upheaval, but she did return to Lesbos. Despite her relative geographical isolation, her fame as a supreme poet quickly spread throughout the Greek and, later, the Roman worlds. We do not know exactly the origins and purpose of her poetic craft; it is likely that she was involved in some kind of educational activities that used poetry to educate adolescent girls. This leads us to the subject of the differences between ancient and modern poetry.

Ancient Poetry as Song

A perceptive reader will have noticed that I refer to Sappho's creations as songs, and this points to the fundamental difference between modern poetry and that of classical antiquity: ancient poems were actually songs performed in public, whereas we tend to read poems silently in private spaces. Instruments such as the lyre or flute accompanied the performer, whether individual or group. We know that Greek poetry in particular was often sung chorally and involved dance as well as music, but scholars today are divided over the extent of choral performances. I have come to believe that virtually all lyric poetry, including Sappho, was performed originally by a chorus. This question is one that all students will have to decide themselves, but it might be at least helpful to imagine the songs sung by individual performers and groups who danced while singing. If the "I" of the songs seems to argue against choral performance, consider that the chorus of a Greek tragedy often speaks as "I," and that imaging the choral performance of Sappho's poems might help you to overcome the stumbling block of integrating the choruses of Greek dramas into the action of the plays (one of the hardest parts of reading Greek tragedy for the first time). Imagining the songs as public choral performances might also help you to see the songs as something other than the spontaneous outbursts of an extremely passionate woman.

Text and Translation

Scanning over the songs below, you will also notice quickly that only one is given the title of song, with the others numbered as fragments. Although we know that Sappho composed thousands of lines of poetry, their numbers were extraordinarily reduced by the ravages of time and by the reaction of Medieval Christians, who objected to her most common subject—love, and especially love between women—and thus burned or erased much of what had survived antiquity. Ancient books were actually scrolls of papyrus, made from reeds found on the Egyptian coast, and which certainly does not wear like marble. Occasionally, new scraps appear from inside pharaohs' tombs, and modern lovers of Sappho's poetry dream of a more substantial scroll emerging from some unfound site under the sands of Egypt. Nonetheless, today we have only a single complete song and a set of fragments. The song, popularly known as "The Hymn to Aphrodite," survives only because an ancient handbook on rhetoric featured it as an example of how to write a great poem!

Thus, in addition to the normal difficulties posed by the Greek language, the translator has to make sense of the gaps in the texts. Whereas many translators of Sappho ignore the gaps, fail to acknowledge them, or compose entirely new sections, I have chosen not to do so. You will read here a fairly literal translation of what Sappho wrote; I use as few words as possible, just as Sappho does, and I do not add metaphors not present in the Greek text. In addition to maintaining brevity, I have tried to communicate the sound play and aural lightness of the songs' sound world. I have also endeavored to keep the same word order and location whenever possible; this results in some English that is not particularly elegant, but it does preserve the flow of images and ideas. A series of dots indicates a break in the manuscript edited by scholars, and brackets indicate words that are incomplete but about which we can make a reasonable, informed guess. A question mark inside a bracket indicates that the guess is less reasonable. Early in "The Hymn to Hector and Andromache" there is a severe enough gap to prevent accurate assessment of a line's meaning, and so there I present an alternative possibility in parentheses. This collection contains most of the substantial fragments attributed to Sappho.

Notes to aid understanding follow at the end of the collection.

Selected Poems

Song (Hymn to Aphrodite)

Throned in many colors, ageless Aphrodite,
daughter of Zeus, wile-weaver, I beg you,
do not with heartbreak and sorrows tame,
Lady, my spirit.

But come here, if ever once at another time
having heard my cries from afar
you then listened, and having left your father's house of
gold, you came

having yoked your chariot; lovely swift sparrows drove
you about the dark earth,
stirring their swift-whirring wings from
Heaven's bright heights
through its middle,

and suddenly they arrived! And you, O blessed one,
smiling with your immortal face,
asked what I have suffered and why
I am calling,

and what for myself I most want to happen
in my maddened spirit; "Whom should I persuade
to lead back to your friendship? Who, O
Sappho treats you unjustly?

For even if she flees, quickly will she pursue;
if she does not receive gifts, instead she will give;
if she does not love, quickly she will love,
even if unwilling."

Come to me also now, and release me from
harsh anxiety, and, as much as my spirit for me
desires to bring to fulfillment, fulfill it. But you
be my ally.

Fragment 1

Some say that a band of cavalry, others one of footsoldiers
still others of ships, on the dark earth is
most beautiful, but I say it's
she the beloved.

Very easy to make understood
is this thing, for she by far sacking in
beauty other humans, her husband—
he the great hero—

she left him to go sailing to Troy,
of child or of dear parents
completely unmindful, but herself was led aside
[by Aphrodite]

. . . lightly . . . .
. . . . .me of Anaktoria delighting . . .

But I would rather see her lovely step
and the bright sparkling of her face
than the chariots of the Lydians and soldiers
all in weapons.

Fragment 2

He seems to me like the gods—
that man whoever facing you

sits and nearby hears
your sweet voice

and lovely laughter, which makes my
heart flutter in my breast;
if I glance at you, how
my tongue can't speak

anymore but is pained, fine
fire flickers beneath my skin
your vision not in my eyes,
my ears abuzz,

then cold sweat drips down me, trembling
captures me completely, greener than grass
am I, to die too weak
I seem to be to myself.
But all is dared and endured . . . .

Fragment 3 (Wedding Hymn for Hector and Andromache)

Oh [goddess of] Cyprus . . . . as
a herald came . . . .
The swift messenger Idaeus spoke these [fine things]
. . . . [line missing]
who sang the undying glory and the other Asian women
[or: whose undying glory stirred the Asian lands]:
"Hector and his companions are leading the quick-glancing girl,
from sacred Thebe and from Plakia [with its fine temples],
the gentle girl Andromache he leads in his ships upon the salt
sea; with them come scores of golden bracelets and cloths of
purple, finely wrought baubles,
countless silver winecups and ivory."
Thus he spoke. Quickly Hector's dear father leapt up;
a rumor came down the city of fair dances to their beloved ones;
immediately the Trojan women were driving forth with fair-wheeled
mule-drawn
carriages, and then the whole crowd of women were
approaching together with the maidens of lovely ankles;
But apart from the rest, Priam's daughters . . .

And men led their chariots under horses,
Children, unmarried youths, and the greatest . . .
charioteers . . . .
. . . .
. . . .
. . . .
. . . . . Men like the gods . . . . .
. . . . Holy all together
sets out . . . . . to [ho]ly Ilium,
a sweet-songed flute and the lyre are mixed in music
with the castanets' clatter, brightly the maidens
sang a holy song, and there came through the air
a god-sent ringing . . . [laughter?] . . . . .
Everywhere on the roads . . . .
Wine-bowls and saucers and w[ine] [fra]grant
Myrrh and cassia and frankincense are mixed.
Women cried out in prayer, so many grandmothers,
and all men were sounding a high lovely song,
invoking Healer Paean, the farshooter, he of the fair lyre,
a hymn for Hector and Andromache the godlike ones.

Fragment 4

Closer to me be, please, while praying,
Lady Hera, your gracious shape,
Which—so prayed for—the Atreids . . .
[Renowned] Kings [saw];

having completed many labors
first around Ilium, then in the sea,
from here having set on the final road
they weren't able to finish their mission,

before calling on you and Zeus who opposed them,
the desirable child of Semele;
now also to me gentle-minded give protection
as you did [long ago?].

Fragment 5

Dead—no lie—I want myself.
She, wailing, was leaving me

And so often said to me this:
"Alas how terribly we have suffered,
Sappho, and now unwillingly I leave you behind."

And I answered her thus:
"Go gladly and remember
me, for you know how we cared for you;

if not, instead I want you
to swear . . . .
. . . and we used to experience beauty.

For coming with many wreaths
of red saffron together with
. . . . . . by me you lay down,

and you threw many braids of
blossoms of thyme
about your soft neck,

and with much myrrh . . .
with perfume made from the rarest flower . . .
you were anointed as if royalty

and upon the bed
so soft . . . .
you would sate your longing . . .

And never would anyone . . . never . . . at all
Nor any temple . . . .
Would have been from which we would have been absent,
Not a grove . . . dancing . . .
Noise . . . .
. . . .

Fragment 6

[much missing at the beginning]
In Sardis . . . .
Often from here having a mind
. . . .
You like an easily recognized
goddess, they much took pleasure in your dancing,

but now it shines among the Lydian women,
like, when the sun sets
the red-fingered moon

surpasses all the stars; light presses
upon the salt sea
and equally upon the many-flowered fields;

and the dew is shed as beauty,
the rose flourishes with the
chervil flowers and blooming clover.
Much wandering,

Remembering with desire
Gentle Atthis,
Her heart is consumed by your fate.

Fragment 7

[opening lines missing]
Here to me, please, from Crete to this temple here
holy, where lie your lovely apple orchards,
and altars fragrant with
frankincense.

Inside, cold water splashes noisily through the
apple branches, and with roses the whole garden is
shaded, and when the leaves quiver enchanted
slumber swoops down.

Inside, the horse-grazed meadow thrives
with Spring's blossoms, and the winds
blow soft.

Yes, here you . . . . ., O Cyprian, taking
in golden goblets gently
pour for our feasts nectar
mixed like wine.

Notes

Hymn to Aphrodite

Aphrodite is the Greek goddess of passionate love, eros. The Greeks imagined two birth myths for her. In the older version found in Hesiod's *Theogony,* Cronos overthrows the first king of the gods, his father Ouranos, by castrating him. From the spot in the sea where the god's genitals land. Aphrodite emerges and steps on to the island of Cyprus; hence Sappho calls her "Cyprian." The second myth has her the child of Zeus and an obscure goddess Dione. Sappho calls Aphrodite "daughter of Zeus," yet frequently refers to Cyprus, so both versions seem to be in play.

The English word "spirit" that appears three times in the poem is a very inadequate translation for the Greek *thumos,* which, although "spirit" forms part of the range of its meanings, also means "passion" or "life force." The Greeks imagined the *thumos* as located in the chest. It is where the gods instill energy and valor into warriors in Homeric epics, and Plato believed it to be the part of us that the reason must tame. Some scholars have argued that this poem is based on the battle cry of warriors in Homer when they are asking for divine assistance.

Fragment I

The second and third stanzas allude to Helen, the great beauty of Greek myth, whose abduction by Paris with the assistance of Aphrodite is the cause of the Trojan War. The phrase, "he the great hero," refers to her husband Menelaus and translates a single Greek term, *panariston,* which literally means "completely the best." This alludes in turn to the ethic of the Homeric heroes whose single desire is to be called the best.

Fragment 3

Hector is the greatest of the warriors in Troy who fight against the Greeks who have come to take back Helen. His death at the hands of Achilles is the climax of Homer's *Iliad*. His relationship with his wife Andromache, whose own father Achilles earlier killed, is depicted in Book 6 of that epic.

At the end of the poem, the Trojans call upon the god Apollo in three of his cult titles: healer, far-shooter (archery), and god of the lyre. All three are also present in the first choral ode of Sophocles' *Oedipus the King*. Apollo fights on the side of the Trojans in the Trojan War.

Fragment 4

Hera is the wife and sister of Zeus, and she serves as goddess of marriage and fertility. Her hatred of the Trojans was implacable.

The Atreids are the two sons of Atreus, Agamemnon and Menelaus.

Semele's child is Dionysus, fathered by Zeus. Dionysus is the Greek god of wine and theater.

Fragment 7

The Cretans claimed Aphrodite came from their island.
Nectar is drunk only by the gods.

Translated and edited by Robin Mitchell-Boyask,
Department of Greek, Roman and Hebrew Classics

The Homeric Hymn to Demeter

Introduction

Homeric Hymns were songs composed, most likely sometime during the 7th century B.C.E., in the style of the Homeric epics, and they told stories of the Olympian gods and other lesser deities. The longer ones preserve important myths from the Archaic Greek world involving how gods came to have certain functions and honors. *The Homeric Hymn to Demeter* is one of the greatest of these texts, renowned for its moving portrayal of a mother's grief over her lost daughter. You might, as a child, have met it in a different form as an explanation of how the seasons originated, but note that this aspect is minimized in this version of the story. You will find its figures and themes resonating in other Greek texts in Intellectual Heritage, as well as in Jewish and Christian readings.

In translation, I aim for as literal a correspondence as I can manage between individual Greek and English words. This has meant preserving the *epithets* (descriptive word combinations, e.g., "slim-ankled" in line 2) attached to the names of the hymn's characters. Epithets mark the hymn's oral origins, because poets used them to fill in lines as formulas while composing the following lines during performances. Sometimes these epithets substitute for the names entirely. The poet of this hymn signals his performance in song in the first and last lines of the hymn. Brackets around certain words indicate places where the surviving manuscripts from the Middle Ages have breaks and gaps that scholars have attempted to fill in with reasonable certainty.

Text

I begin to sing of fair-haired Demeter, the revered goddess,
And her slim-ankled daughter[1] whom Aïdoneus[2]
Grabbed, and whom deep-thundering, broad-faced Zeus gave,
Far from Demeter of the golden sword and shining fruit,
As she was playing with the daughter of Okeanos,
    with their gowns of deep folds,   5
Plucking flowers of red and saffron and lovely violet
In the soft meadow, iris and hyacinth
And narcissus, which as a deception for the flower-faced girl,
Gaia[3] grew by the plans of Zeus, doing a favor for the Receiver-of-Many,
A deception gleaming wonderfully, an awesome sight for all   10
The deathless gods and mortal human beings.
And from its root a hundred-blossomed head grew out,
And the sweetest aroma gave scent, and all broad heaven above
And all the earth laughed, and all the briny swell of the sea.
She, amazed, stretched out with both hands   15
To seize the lovely delight as if a plaything; and the broad-pathed earth
Yawned open on the Nysian plain where the lord, Receiver-of-Many,
The many-named son of Kronos[4] rushed with his deathless horses.
Grabbing her, unwilling upon the golden chariots
He drove her, crying in laments; she shrieked up to the sky with her voice,   20
Calling on her father the son of Kronos, the supreme and best.
And nobody of the immortal ones nor of mortal human beings
Heard her voice, nor did the olive trees with their shining fruit,
Except that the daughter of Persaios, thinking tenderly,
Hekatê of the soft veil, perceived it from her cave,   25
And the lord Helios, shining son of Hyperion,
Heard the girl calling on her father the son of Kronos; and he far away
From the gods sat above in his temple sought with many prayers,
Receiving fine sacred things from mortal human beings.
At the suggestion of Zeus he drove her against her will,   30
He her father's brother, Commander-of-Many, Receiver-of-Many,
The many-named son of Kronos with the deathless horses.
As long as the goddess still beheld earth
And starry heaven and the swift-flowing fish-filled sea
And the rays of the sun, she still hoped she would see her cherished mother   35
And the tribes of the eternal gods,
While hope still charmed her great mind, although she felt great pain;

The mountain peaks and sea depths echoed
Under her immortal voice, which her regal mother heard.
Sharp pain seized her heart, and the scarf about her ambrosial 40
Hair she tore with her own hands,
And threw a deep purple veil about both shoulders,[5]
And rushed like a bird over land and water,
Searching; and no one, neither of gods nor of mortal human beings
Wished to speak a true word to her, 45
Nor did one of the birds come as a true messenger.
For nine days then on the land did regal Deô,[6]
Turn about constantly, holding burning torches,
And in her grief tasted neither ambrosia nor sweet-drinking nectar,[7]
Nor did she she wash her skin with water. 50
But when the the tenth appearance of gleaming Dawn arrived,
Hekatê met her, holding a flame in her own hands,
And as a messenger spoke a word and addressed her:

"Regal Demeter, season-bringer, one with shiny gifts,
who of heavenly gods or of mortal human beings 55
grabbed Persephonê and broke your dear heart?
For I heard a voice, but I did not see with my eyes
Whoever it was; so with speed to you I say all unerringly."

Thus did Hekatê speak; but the fair-haired daughter of Rhea
Did not answer her with a word, but swiftly with her 60
She sped, holding burning torches with her hands.
They reached Helios, watcher of the gods and of men,
And standing before his horses the bright goddess said:

"Helios, please have respect for me as a goddess, if ever
I have cheered your heart and spirit with word or deed. 65
A girl whom I bore, a sweet child, noble in form,
Whose loud voice I heard through the fruitless air,
As if she were being forced, but I did not see with my eyes.
But since you look down with your rays from the bright air
upon the whole earth and sea 70
Please tell me truly if you have seen my dear child somewhere
Or who of the gods or of mortal human beings
Has gone, and has taken her unwillingly far from me, under compulsion."

Thus she spoke, and the son of Hyperion answered her with a word:

"Daughter of fair-haired Rhea, my lady Demeter,   75
you will know; for I hold you greatly in awe and I pity
you in grief for your slim-ankled daughter. But none other of
the immortals is responsible save cloud-gathering Zeus,
who gave her to his brother Hades to be called his flower-fresh
bedmate; but he, having grabbed her,   80
with his horses drove her screaming under the murky gloom.
But, goddess, stop your great lament; you must not
In vain hold such an unapproachable rage. For not unsuitable
A son-in-law among the immortals is Aïdoneus, Commander-of-Many,
Your brother of the same seed; he has received an honored share   85
When the first three-way division of the spoils occurred.[8]
He is the ruler of those who share his dwelling."

Thus having spoken, he called to his horses, and at his call
They lightly bore his swift chariot like slender-winged birds.
But a pain sharper and biting like a dog came to her spirit.   90
Enraged, then, at the dark-clouded son of Kronos,
Turning her back on the assembly of the gods and great Olympus
She went to the cities of men and their rich deeds,
Disguising her shape for a long time. And no one of men
Or of deep-girdled women, recognized her at sight until   95
When she came to the home of prudent Keleus,
Who then was the ruler of Eleusis, fragrant with incense.
She sat near the road, her dear heart wasting away
At the well of the Virgin, from which the townspeople drew water
In shadow, but olive grew thick above it,   100
And she looked like an old woman born long ago, and who was barred
From childbirth and the gifts of lovely-crowned Aphrodite,
And such are the nurses of law-giving kings
And the housekeepers about their echoing houses.
The daughters of Keleus of Eleusis saw her   105
When they came to bring the easily drawn water
With bronze pitchers to the dear house of their father,
Holding their maiden's bloom like four goddesses,
Kallidikê and Kleisidikê and lovely Dêmô
And Kallithoê, who was the first born of them all;   110
But they did not recognize her. Gods are difficult for mortals to see.
Standing near they spoke winged words to her:

"Who among the ancient people are you, old woman, and where are you from?"

Why do you keep yourself far from the city and do not approach   115
The houses? There are women the same age as you
Throughout the shady halls and some who are younger,
Who would welcome you warmly, both in word and in deed."
Thus she spoke, and the queen among goddesses answered with words:

"Dear children, whoever you are among women,   120
greetings, and I will tell you my story. It is not unseemly
to tell you a true story to you when you are asking.
Dôs is my name, which my regal mother gave to me;
Now from Krete upon the broad back of the sea
I have come, against my will, for pirate men   125
Led me off unwillingly under violent compulsion. Then they
With their swift ship put in at Thorikon, where women
Stepped onto the land in a crowd and the men
Prepared their dinner at the prow of the ship;
But my spirit did not desire a pleasant dinner,   130
So in secret setting forth through the black earth
I fled my arrogant commanders, so that they could not
export me, penniless, for sale, and have use of my honor.
Thus I have come here, wandering, and I do not know at all
What land this is and whoever lives here.   135
But may all those holding the Olympian homes
Give you husbands in marriage and children to bear
As your parents wish; but, girls, please pity me in turn
So that I may come with good thoughts to your children,[9]
And the house of a man and his wife, so that I may work for them
Thoughtfully in such jobs as are appropriate for a woman of my age.   140
And holding the newborn child in my arms
I would nurse him beautifully and watch over the house
And make the master's bed in a recess of the well-built chambers
And I would teach the works of a woman."

The goddess spoke. And the unwedded maiden, Kallidikê,   145
The best in appearance of the daughters of Keleus, answered her:

"Good mother, gifts of the gods we human beings endure even when
we are aggrieved by necessity; for, indeed, they are more powerful by far.
But I will declare clearly to you and name
The men for whom there is great power of honor here,   150
And who are the leaders of the people, and by whose counsels

And straight acts of justice the city's ramparts are guarded.[10]
We are wives who manage the households of all these men:
Shrewd Triptolemos and Dioklos
And Dolichos and of our own kingly father;
And all of these have wives who manage their households.   155
None of us would at first sight
Turn you away from our homes and dishonor your appearance,
But all will welcome you; for certainly you look like a god.
If you wish, remain there, so that we might go to father's house   160
And we might speak to our deep-girdled mother Metaneira
Of all these matters thoroughly, if she might command you
To go to our house and not seek the houses of others.
An only child, her son, late-born, is being raised
In our well-built palace, a son after many prayers and welcome.   165
If you could raise him and he might reach the measure of adolescence,
Any one of the race of female woman, having seen you,
Might become jealous; and such gifts mother might give you for caring."

Thus she spoke, and the other woman nodded with her head in assent,
         and the girls,
After filling their gleaming vessels with water, carried them off, rejoicing.   170
Swiftly they came to the great house of their father, and quickly they told
Their mother what they saw and heard. And she very quickly
Ordered them, though already willing, to invite her for pay without limit.
And they, like deer or heifers in the season of spring,
Bounded through the meadow, satisfying their hearts with food,   175
So they, grasping the folds of their lovely fine robes,
Sped in their hollow wagon, and their hair about their
Shoulders flew back like a saffron blossom.
They overtook the noble goddess near the road in the very place where
They had left her before. And then to the dear house of their father   180
They led her, and she, wasting away in her own dear heart,
Came behind, a veil covering her head, and a deep purple robe
Swirled about the slender feet of the goddess.
Swiftly they reached the house of god-nurtured Keleus,
And they went through the corridor where their regal mother   185
Sat by a column of the thickly built roof,
Holding her young child under her breast; and they ran
To her, but the goddess went to the threshold with her feet,
Her head touched the roof, and the doorway filled with goddess glow.
Shame and reverence and green fear seized the mother;   190

She withdrew from the couch and urged the other to sit down.
But, no, Demeter of the gleaming gifts, season-bringer,
Did not want to sit upon the radiant couch,
But she remained, grieving, casting down her beautiful eyes,
Until prudent, knowing Iambê set out   195
A sturdy stool, and over it threw a bright silver fleece.
Sitting there she held a veil in front of her face;
She sat on the stool for a long time, unspeaking, wasting away,
And she responded to nobody at all with word or act,
But unlaughing, not tasting food or drink   200
She sat ever-shrinking because of longing for her deep-girdled daughter,
Until prudent, knowing Iambê, jesting much around her
Turned her, regal and holy,
To smile and to laugh and to keep a gentle spirit;
And Iambê kept pleasing her moods even later.   205
For the goddess Metaneira filled and gave a cup
Of honey-sweet wine, but she refused it; for it is not permitted, she said,
For her to drink red wine, and she compelled her to give a drink
Mixed of water mixed with barley and soft mint.
Metaneira made the drink[11] and gave it to the goddess as she had ordered.   210
Receiving it for the sake of sacred law, regal Dêô . . .

[There is a gap in the text here.]

To them Metaneira of the fair girdle began her words:

"Greetings, lady! For I suppose that you come not from bad parents
but from noble ones. A sense of shame and grace are
visible in your eyes as if you were indeed from one of the law-giving kings.   215
But by necessity we human beings endure the gifts of the gods
Even in our grief; for the yoke lies upon our neck.[12]
But now since you have come here, you will have such things as are mine.
Nurture the boy you see here, late-born and beyond hope
Have the immortals given him to us, but he was much-prayed for by me.   220
If you could nurture him and he could come to the measure of adolescence,
Any one of the race of female woman, having seen you,
Might become jealous; and such gifts I would give you for caring."

In turn fair-crowned Demeter addressed her:

"And greetings to you too, lady, and may the gods give you good things.   225

I will thoughtfully receive your boy as you urge me;
I will nurture him, and I do not suppose that by the foolishness of his nurse
Nor by witchcraft nor by the Undercutter[13] will he be harmed;
For I know an antidote much stronger than the Woodcutter,
And I know a good safeguard against witchcraft."   230

Thus having spoken, she received the child to her fragrant breast
And her immortal hands; and his mother rejoiced in her mind.
So she reared in the palace the shining son of prudent Keleus,
Dêmophoön, whom fair-girdled Metaneira had borne.
And he grew equal to a god   235
Eating no food nor sucking [the breast of his mother
For by day fair-crowned divine] Demeter
Anointed him[14] with ambrosia as if he had been born from a god,
Breathing sweetly on him and holding him to her breasts.
Each night she hid him like a firebrand in the flame's power,
In secret from his dear parents; and to them there was a great wonder   240
As he grew very fast and he seemed like the gods.
And she would have made him ageless and immortal
If fair-girdled Metaneira had not in her foolishness
One night spied out from her fragrant chamber
And saw for herself.[15] She shrieked and struck both thighs,   245
Fearing for her child and struck with a great delusion in her heart,[16]
And crying out she spoke winged words:

"My child Dêmophoön, the stranger hides you in much fire,
and in me she places weeping and bitter cares."

Thus she spoke, wailing, and the great one among goddesses heard her.   250
Enraged at her, fair-crowned Demeter snatched from the fire
the dear boy, whom the other had borne beyond hope in the palace,
and with her immortal hands she placed him on the ground
feeling tremendous anger,
and at the same time she addressed fair-girdled Metaneira: 255

"Human beings are fools and senseless, unable to recognize
their appointed lot of good and evil that approaches them
for you too were greatly deluded in your foolishness.
Let the oath of the gods, the implacable water of Styx[17] witness that
I would have made your boy immortal and deathless through all his days,   260
And I would have given him honor that does not wither away.

But now it is impossible that he escape death and the goddesses of death.[18]
He will always have honor that does not wither away because upon my knees
He came and in my arms he slept.
But when the years roll around with the seasons   265
The sons of the Eleusinians will conduct war
And the dire battle-cry with each other through all their days.
I am Demeter, bearer of honor, who is
The greatest source of help and joy for both immortals and mortals.
But come now and let all the people build me a great temple and   270
An altar under it, under the city and the high wall
Upon the rising hill of Kallichoros;
I myself shall lay down my rites so that then
Performing due rites you might propitiate my spirit."

Thus having spoken, the goddess changed her size and form,   275
And shoved off old age, and beauty was fragrant around her.
And a lovely scent was scattered from her
Fragrant robes, and, far off, light shone from the immortal skin
Of the goddess, and tawny hair flowed down her shoulders,
And the sturdy house was filled with shining light as if from lightning.   280
And she departed the palace, but the other one's knees went slack,
And for a long time she lost her voice, nor did at all
She remember to lift her only son from the floor.
His sisters heard his pitiful voice,
And bore him to his comfortable bed; and then one   285
Took him up in her hands and pressed him close to her breast,
And another kindled the fire, and another sped with her soft feet
To stir their mother from the fragrant chamber.
Gathering up the wheezing child they bathed
And fondled him; but his heart was not soothed.   290
For lesser caregivers and nurses now held him.
And all night they propitiated the mighty goddess,
Shaking with fear; and as soon as dawn appeared,
They told the true story to Keleus, broad in his power,
As the goddess, fair-crowned Demeter had ordered.   295
And so he called to assembly his boundless people
And compelled them to make a rich temple
For fair-haired Demeter upon the rising hill.
And they very quickly obeyed and heeded his speech,
And they made it as he had ordered; and it grew as by the
        decree of the goddess.   300

But when they had brought this to fulfillment and rested from labor,
Each of them went to go homewards; but golden-haired Demeter,
Sitting there far from the all the blessed ones,
Remained wasting away with longing for her deep-girdled daughter.
And upon the all-nourishing earth she made the year extremely dire   305
And most brutal[19] for mortals, nor did the earth at all
Release her seed; for fair-crowned Demeter kept it hidden.
And in vain oxen dragged many plows in the fields,
And much white barley fell uselessly upon the earth.
And then she would have destroyed the entire race of men
      endowed with speech   310
By grievous famine, and she would have deprived those who keep
Homes on Olympus of their glorious honor of gifts and sacrifices,
Had Zeus not recognized this and pondered it in his heart.
He first stirred gold-winged Iris[20] to summon
Fair-haired Demeter who holds such a lovely form.   315
Thus he spoke. And she obeyed dark-clouded Zeus
And ran swiftly with her feet through the space between earth and heaven.
She reached the city of fragrant Eleusis,
And found dark-robed Demeter in her temple,
And she addressed her, speaking winged words: 320

"Demeter, Father Zeus, who knows the things that do not fade away,
Invites you to come to the tribes of the eternal gods.
But, come! Do not let my word from Zeus be unfulfilled."

Thus she spoke, beseeching her, but the other one's heart was not persuaded.
In turn then the father sent all the eternally blessed gods,   325
And coming one-by-one, they kept imploring her,
Giving her many splendid gifts,
And telling what honors among the immortals she might wish to choose;
But no one was able to persuade the thoughts or mind
Of her, raging in her spirit, and she harshly rejected their speeches.   330
And she kept saying that never would she set foot upon
Fragrant Olympus, nor would she release the fruit from the earth,
Until she could see with her own eyes her fair-faced daughter.
But when deep-thundering, broad-faced Zeus heard this,
He sent to Erebus[21] the slayer of Argus with his wand of gold,[22]   335
So that by cajoling Hades with soft words
He might lead back from the misty gloom to the light
holy Persephonê among the gods, and so that her mother,

seeing her with her own eyes, might withdraw from her rage.
And Hermes did not obey, and speeding under the depths of the earth,   340
He rushed downwards and left the seat of Olympus.
He met the lord Hades inside his house,
Sitting on his couch with his respectful spouse
Who was grieving much in longing for her mother. But she in turn
[Craftily plotted revenge for the deeds of the blessed gods.]   345
And standing near, the strong slayer of Argus spoke:

"Dark-haired Hades, ruling over the dead,
Father Zeus compels me to lead out from Erebus
Noble Persephonê with us, so that her mother,
Seeing her with her own eyes, might cease from her   350
Rage and wrath against the immortals; since she plots a great task
To destroy the helpless tribes of earth-born human beings
By hiding the seed under the earth, and thus obliterating the honors
Of the immortals. She keeps a dire rage, nor with the gods
Does she mingle, but far off in her fragrant temple   355
She sits, keeping the rocky city of Eleusis."

Thus he spoke. And the lord of the Underworld, Aïdoneus smiled
With his eyebrows, and did not disobey the orders of King Zeus.
He swiftly commanded to prudent Persephonê:

"Persephonê, go to your dark-robed mother's side   360
keeping a gentle spirit and heart,
don't keep an ill temper in your heart beyond the others.
But, as the brother of father Zeus I would not be an unseemly
Husband among the immortals; and being here
Your rule over all who live and walk the earth,   365
Possessing the greatest honors among the immortals,
And, for all days, there will be vengeance against those committing injustice,
Whoever does not not propitiate your spirit with sacrifices,
Piously making proper gifts in fulfillment of their duties."

Thus he spoke. And prudent Persephonê rejoiced,   370
Leaping up suddenly for joy; but he himself
Gave her a honey-sweet seed of a pomegranate, stealthily
Guiding it around her, lest she remain all her days
Again by reverent, dark-robed Demeter.
And then Aïdoneus, ruler of many, yoked his   375

Immortal horses to his golden chariot.
She mounted the chariot, and beside her the strong slayer of Argus
Took the reins and the whip with his own hands
And sped them from the palace. And the horse pair flew along not unwillingly.
And they reached the end of their long journey, and neither sea   380
Or the water of rivers nor the grassy meadows
Nor the mountain tops restrained the charge of the immortal horses,
But over them they cut through the deep air in their journey.
Leading them along, he stood them where fair-crowned Demeter remained
Before the fragrant temple. And she, having caught sight of them   385
Sped like a maenad[23] down a mountain shaded with woods.
Persephonê, when she saw [the lovely eyes of her mother
from the other side], left behind the chariot and horses
and leapt to run, and fell in embrace on the neck of her mother;
but while [she held her dear daughter in her hands]   390
her heart quic[kly sensed some guile and she shrank back in fear,]
withdra[wing from their loving embrace, she immediately asked:]

"Child, can you tell me whether you [tasted any] food [while you were below]?
Speak you, and [don't hide anything, so that we might both know.]
For, if not, then returning [from hateful Hades]   395
You could live with me and father, the dark-[clouded son of Kronos,]
With honor from all [the immortals.]
But, if you have, then you, having eaten, must return under
        [the caverns of the earth]
And you will live there a third share of the seasons [each year],
And the other two with me and the [other immort]als.   400
Whenever the earth flourishes with fragrant spring-[time blossoms]
Of every sort, then from the gloomy mist
Again you will arise as a great wonder for gods and mortal human beings.
By what guile did the powerful Receiver-of-Many deceive you?"

And then lovely Persephonê spoke in response to her: 405

"I will tell you the whole truth, mother;
The swift messenger, luck-bringing Hermes came to me
From father, the son of Kronos and from the other heavenly ones,
That I should depart from Erebus, so that, having seen me with your own eyes
You might withdraw from your rage and dire wrath against
        the immortals,   410
But, when I leapt up for joy, he in turn stealthily

Gave to me the honey-sweet seed of a pomegranate,
And he compelled me by force, against my will, to eat it.
But then how, having seized me on account of the strong cunning of
    the son of Kronos,
My father, he went carrying me under the caverns of the earth,   415
This I will explain and I will go through all as you ask.
We all were in the lovely meadow,
Leukippê and Phainô and êlektra and Ianthê
And Melitê and Iachê and Rhodeia and Kalliroê
And Mêlobosis and Tuchê and lovely-faced ôkuroê   420
And Chrysêïs and Ianeira and Akastê and Admêtê
And Rhodopê and Ploutô and charming Kalypsô
And Styx and Ouraniê and lovely Galaxaurê
And Pallas rousing the fight and Artemis shooter of arrows,
All of us were playing and we were plucking the lovely flowers
    with our hands,   425
A mix of soft crocus and irises and hyacinth
And rose-buds and lilies, a wonder to behold,
And narcissus that the broad earth grew as if it were crocus.
But I plucked it with joy and the earth from below
Gaped open, and from it leapt out the powerful lord, Receiver-of-Many.   430
And he departed under the earth in his golden chariot, carrying me
Very much against my will, and I shouted to the heights with my voice.
Though feeling grief at these things, I still tell them all truthfully."

Thus then, throughout the whole day, holding a spirit of a single mind,
They much soothed the heart and spirit of one another,   435
Embracing each other, and each spirit ceased from pain.
And they received and gave joy to each other.
Hekatê of the bright head band came near to them,
And she embraced warmly the daughter of holy Demeter;
From this time she became her attendant and mistress of her companions.   440
To them deep-thundering, broad-faced Zeus sent as a go-between
Fair-haired Rhea,[24] to bring the dark-robed mother
Among the tribes of the gods, and he promised to give her
Honors, whichever ones she might choose among the immortal gods.
He has approved that his daughter should spend a third of the year,   445
As it rolls around, under the misty gloom,
And the other two parts by her mother and the other immortals.
Thus he spoke; and the goddess did not disobey the messages of Zeus.
Swiftly she sped down from the peaks of Olympus,

And she arrived at the Rarion plain, which before had been   450
The life-bringing udder of the earth, but then it was no longer fertile,
But stood fallow and devoid of leaves; for the white barley was hidden
By the plans of fair-ankled Demeter. But very soon,
As spring time increased, it would wave with long ears of grain
And the rich furrows would grow heavy with grain   455
Which would be bound up as sheaves.
And there she first landed from the barren air;
They saw each other with pleasure and rejoiced in their spirit.
Thus Rhea of the soft veil addressed her:

"Come here, child, deep-thundering, broad-faced Zeus invites you   460
to come among the tribes of gods, and promises to give you
[honors, whichever you would like,] among the immortal gods.
[He has approved that his daughter should spend a] third of the year,
[As it rolls around,] under the misty gloom,
[And the other two parts by her mother and the other] immortals.   465
[It is ful]filled as he said and he has nodded with his head
But, come, my child, and obey, and not too much
So [incessantly] should you rage at the dark-clouded son of Kronos.
Im[mediately provide] that the fruit become fertile for human beings."

Thus [she spoke, and fair-crowned Demeter did not disobey,]   470
But immediately she released the fruit of the bountiful fields.
And all the broad earth was heavy with leaves and blossoms.
She went to the law-giving kings,
Triptolemos and horse-driving Diokles,
Strong Eumolpos and Keleus, leader of the people,   475
And she revealed the care of her sacred things and her rites to them all,
Both to Triptolemos and to Polyxeinos, and in addition to them Diokles,
Holy rites, which are not possible at all to be transgressed, [nor to
        inquire about],
Nor to speak aloud; for a reverence of the gods constrains the voice.
Blessed is he of men on earth who has seen these things;   480
But he who is unititiated into the sacred things, who lacks a share in them,
He never has the same destiny when dead under the misty gloom.[25]
But when the queen among goddesses completed the foundations,
She went to go to Olympus among the company of the other gods.
And there the goddesses dwell by Zeus who rejoices in lightning,   485
Holy and reverent. And he of men on earth is greatly blessed whom
They graciously love.

And soon they send to the hearth of his great house
Ploutos, who gives wealth to mortal human beings
But, come, goddesses, holding the people of fragrant Eleusis,   490
And sea-girt Paros and rocky Antron,
Mistress Dêô, lady, bringer of seasons
Herself and her beautiful daughter Persephone,
Graciously in exchange for my song grant a heart-warming living.
For I shall remember both you and another song.

Map 3-5: Classical Greece.

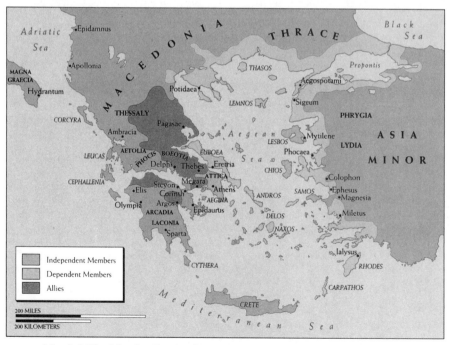

Map 3-6: The Athenian Empire about 450 B.C.E.

Begun in 431 B.C.E. (Translated by Richard Crawley, updated and edited by R. Mitchell-Boyask. Selections from Book 2: Second Year of the War.)

Thucydides: The History of the Peloponnesian War

Funeral Speech of Pericles

34. In the same winter the Athenians gave a funeral at public cost to the first who had fallen in this war. It was a custom of their ancestors, according to the following manner. Three days before the ceremony, the bones of the dead are laid out in a tent which has been erected; and their friends bring to their relatives such offerings as they please. In the funeral procession, cypress coffins are carried in cars, one for each tribe; the bones of the deceased being placed in the coffin of their tribe. Among these is carried one empty bier decked for the missing, that is, for those whose bodies could not be recovered. Any citizen or stranger who pleases joins in the procession; and the female relatives are there to wail at the burial. The dead are laid in the public sepulcher in the beautiful suburb of the city, in which those who fall in war are always buried; with the exception of those slain at Marathon, who for their singular and extraordinary valor were interred on the spot where they fell. After the bodies have been laid in the earth, a man chosen by the state, of recognized wisdom and eminent reputation, pronounces over them an appropriate panegyric, after which all retire. Such is the manner of the burying; and throughout the whole of the war, whenever the occasion arose, the established custom was observed. Meanwhile these were the first that had fallen, and Pericles, son of Xanthippus, was chosen to pronounce their eulogy. When the proper time arrived, he advanced from the sepulcher to an elevated platform in order to be heard by as many of the crowd as possible, and spoke as follows:

35. "Most of my predecessors here have commended him who made this speech part of the law, telling us that it is well that it should be delivered at the burial of those who fall in battle. For myself, I should have thought that the worth which had displayed itself in deeds would be sufficiently rewarded by honors also shown by deeds; such as you now see in this funeral prepared at the people's cost. And I could have wished that the reputations of many brave men were not to be imperiled in the mouth of a single individual, to stand or fall according as he spoke well or ill. For it is hard to speak properly upon a subject where it is even difficult to convince your hearers that you are speaking the truth. On the one hand, the friend who is familiar with every fact of the story may think that some point has not been set forth with that fullness which he wishes and knows it to deserve; on the other, he who is a stranger to the matter may be led by envy to suspect exaggeration if he hears anything above his own nature. For men can endure to hear others praised only so long as they can each persuade themselves of their own ability to equal the actions recounted: when this point is passed, envy comes in and with it incredulity. However, since our ancestors have stamped this custom with their approval, it becomes my duty to obey the law and to try to satisfy your several wishes and opinions as best I may.

36. "I shall begin with our ancestors: it is both just and proper that they have the honor of the first mention on an occasion like the present. They lived in this country continuously from generation to generation, and handed it down free to the present time by their valor. And if our more remote ancestors deserve praise, much more do our own fathers, who added to their inheritance the empire which we now possess, and spared no pains to be able to leave their acquisitions to us of the present generation. Lastly, there are few parts of our dominions that we here have not increased, we who are still more or less in the vigor of life; while the city has been made self-sufficient for war or for peace. That part of our history which tells of the military achievements which gave us our various possessions, or of the ready valor with which either we or our fathers stemmed the tide of Hellenic or foreign aggression, is a theme too familiar to my hearers for me to explain, and I shall therefore pass it by. But what was the road by which we reached our position, what the form of government under which our greatness grew, what the national habits out of which it sprang; these are questions which I may try to answer before I proceed to my panegyric upon these men; since I think this to be a subject upon which on the present occasion a speaker may properly dwell, and to which the whole assembly, whether citizens or foreigners, may profitably listen.

37. "Our constitution does not copy the laws of neighboring states; we are rather a model to others than imitators ourselves. Its administration favors the many instead of the few; this is why it is called a democracy. Our laws afford equal justice to all in their private differences; lacking social standing, advancement in public life falls to reputation for ability, class considerations not being allowed to interfere with merit. Nor again does poverty bar the way, if a man is able to serve the state, he is not hindered by the obscurity of his condition. The freedom which we enjoy in our government extends also to our ordinary life. There, mindful of, but not jealously spying on, each other, we do not feel called upon to be angry with our neighbor for doing what he likes, or even to indulge in those injurious looks which are always offensive, although not harmful. But all this ease in our private relations does not make us lawless as citizens. Against this, fear is our chief safeguard, teaching us to obey the magistrates and the laws, particularly such as regard the protection of the injured, whether they are actually on the statute book, or belong to that code which, although unwritten, yet cannot be broken without public shame.

38. "Further, we regularly refresh our minds by celebrating games and festivals all the year round, and the elegance of our private establishments forms a daily source of pleasure and helps to banish fatigue; while the magnitude of our city draws the merchandise of the world into our harbor, so that to the Athenian the fruits of other countries are as familiar a luxury as those of his own.

39. "We differ from our antagonist also in our military policy. We throw open our city to the world, and never expel foreigners from any opportunity of learning or observing, although the eyes of an enemy may occasionally profit by our liberality; trusting less in system and policy than to the native spirit of our citizens; while in education, where our rivals from their very cradles by a painful discipline pursue manliness, at Athens we live exactly as we please, and yet are just as ready to encounter every legitimate danger. In proof of this it may be noticed that the Lacedaemonians do not invade our country alone, but bring with them all their allies; while we Athenians advance alone into the territory of a neighbor, and fighting upon a foreign soil usually vanquish with ease men who are defending their homes. Our united force was never yet encountered by any enemy, because we have at once to attend to our navy and to dispatch our citizens by land upon a hundred different services; so that, wherever they engage with some such fraction of our strength, a success against a detachment is magnified into a victory over the nation, and a defeat into a reverse suffered at the hands of our entire people. And yet if with habits not of labor but of ease, and courage not taught but natural, we are still willing to encounter danger, we have the double advantage of escaping the experience of hardships in anticipation and effacing them in the hour of need as fearlessly as those who are never free from them.

Nor are these the only points in which our city is worthy of admiration.

40. "We cultivate refinement without extravagance and knowledge without effeminacy; wealth we employ more for use than for show, and place the real disgrace of poverty not in admitting it but in not fighting against it. Our public men have, besides politics, their private affairs to attend to, and our ordinary citizens, though occupied with the pursuits of industry, are still fair judges of public matters; for, unlike any other nation, we regard him who takes no part in these duties not as unambitious but as useless. We Athenians thus are able to decide on policy and have proper debates about it, and, instead of looking on discussion as a stumbling-block in the way of action, we think it an indispensable preliminary to any wise action at all. Again, in our enterprises we present the singular spectacle of daring and deliberation, each carried to its highest point, and both united in the same persons; although usually decision is the fruit of ignorance, hesitation of reflection. But the badge of courage will surely be awarded most justly to those, who best know the difference between hardship and pleasure and yet are never tempted to shrink from danger. In generosity we are equally singular, acquiring our friends by conferring, not by receiving, favors. Yet, of course, the doer of the favor is the firmer friend of the two, in order by continued kindness to keep the recipient in his debt; while the debtor feels less keenly from the very consciousness that the return he makes will be a payment, not a free gift. And it is only the Athenians, who, fearless of consequences, confer their benefits not from calculations of expediency, but in the confidence of generosity.

41. "In short, I say that as a city we are the school of Greece, while I doubt if the world can produce a self-sufficient man who is equal to so many emergencies, and graced by so happy a versatility, as the Athenian. And that this is no mere boast thrown out for the occasion, but plain matter of fact, the power of the state acquired by these habits proves. For Athens alone of her peers is found when tested to surpass her reputation, and alone gives no occasion to her opponents to feel shame at their defeat, or to her subjects to question her title by merit to rule. Rather, the admiration of the present and succeeding ages will be ours, since we have not left our power without witness, but have shown it by mighty proofs; and far from needing a Homer for our panegyrist, or other of his craft whose verses might charm for the moment only for the impression which they gave to melt at the touch of fact, we have forced every sea and land to be the highway of our daring, and everywhere, whether for evil or for good, have left imperishable monuments behind us. Such is the Athens for which these men, in the assertion of their resolve not to lose her, nobly fought and died; and well may every one of their survivors be ready to suffer in her cause.

42. "Indeed if I have dwelt at some length upon the character of our country, it has been to show that our stake in the struggle is not the same as theirs who have no such blessings to lose, and also that the panegyric of the men over whom I am now speaking might be by definite proofs established. That panegyric is now in a great measure complete; for the Athens that I have celebrated is only what the heroism of these and their like have made her, men whose fame, unlike that of most Hellenes, will be found to be only commensurate with their rewards. And if a test of worth be wanted, it is to be found in their final act, and this not only in cases in which it set the final seal upon their merit, but also in those in which it gave the first intimation of their having any. For there is justice in the claim that steadfastness in his country's battles should be as a cloak to cover a man's other imperfections; since

the good action has blotted out the bad, and his virtue as a citizen more than out-weighed his vices as an individual. But none of these allowed either wealth with its prospect of future enjoyment to unnerve his spirit, or poverty with its hope of a day of freedom and riches to tempt him to shrink from danger. No, holding that vengeance upon their enemies was more to be desired than any personal blessings, and reck-oning this to be the most glorious of hazards, they joyfully determined to accept the risk, to make sure of their vengeance, and to let their wishes wait; and while committing to hope the uncertainty of final success, in the business before them they thought fit to act boldly and trust in themselves. Thus choosing to die resist-ing, rather than to live submitting, they fled only from dishonor, but met danger head on, and after one brief moment, while at the peak of their fortune, escaped, not from their fear, but from their glory.

43. "These men were worthy of their city. You, their survivors, must deter-mine to have as altering a resolve in the field, though you may pray that it may have a happier outcome. And not contented with ideas derived only from words of the advantages which are bound up with the defense of your country, though these would furnish a valuable text to a speaker even before an audience so alive to them as the present, you must yourselves realize the power of Athens, and feast your eyes upon her from day to day, till you become her dedicated lover; and then, when all her great-ness shall dawn upon you, you must reflect that it was by courage, sense of duty, and a keen feeling of honor in action that men were enabled to win all this, and that no personal failure in an enterprise could make them consent to deprive their country of their valor, but they laid it at her feet as the most glorious contribution that they could offer. For this offering of their lives made in common by them all they each of them individually received that renown which never grows old, and for a sepulcher, not so much that in which their bones have been deposited, but that noblest of shrines wherein their glory is laid up to be eternally remembered upon every occasion on which deed or story shall call for its commemoration. For heroes have the whole earth for their tomb; and in lands far from their own, where the column with its epi-taph declares it, there is enshrined in every breast a record unwritten with no tablet to preserve it, except that of the heart. These take as your model and, judging that happiness depends on freedom and freedom depends on courage, never decline the dangers of war. For it is not the miserable that would most justly be unsparing of their lives; these have nothing to hope for: it is rather they to whom continued life may bring obstacles as yet unknown, and to whom a fall, if it came, would be most tremendous in its consequences. And surely, to a man of spirit, the degradation of cowardice must be immeasurably more harmful than the unfelt death which strikes him in the midst of his strength and patriotism!

44. "Comfort, therefore, not condolence, is what I have to offer to the par-ents of the dead who may be here. Numberless are the chances to which, as they know, the life of man is subject; but fortunate indeed are they who draw for their lot a death so glorious as that which has caused your mourning, and to whom life has been so exactly measured as to terminate in the happiness in which it has been passed. Still I know that this is a harsh thought, especially when those are in question of whom you will constantly be reminded by seeing in the homes of others blessings of which once you also boasted: for grief is felt not so much for the want of what we have never known, as for the loss of that to which we have been long accustomed. Yet you who are still of an age to beget children must bear up in the hope of having others in their place; not only will they help you to forget those whom you have lost, but will be to the state at once a reinforcement and a security; for never can a fair or just policy be expected of the citizen who does not, like his fellows, bring to the decision the interests and apprehensions of a father. While those of you who have passed your prime must congratulate yourselves with the thought that the best part of your life was fortunate, and that the brief span that remains will be cheered by the fame of the departed. For it is only the love of honor that never grows old; and honor it is, not gain, as some would have it, that rejoices the heart of age and helplessness.

45. "Turning to the sons or brothers of the dead, I see an arduous struggle before you. When a man is gone, all are wont to praise him, and should your merit be ever so transcendent, you will still find it difficult not merely to overtake, but even to approach their renown. The living have envy to contend with, while those who are no longer in our path are honored with a goodwill into which rivalry does not enter. On the other hand, if I must say anything on the subject of female excellence to those of you who will now be in widowhood, it will be all comprised in this brief exhortation. Great will be your glory in not falling short of your natural character; and greatest will be hers who is least talked of among the men, whether for good or for bad.

46. "My task is now finished. I have performed it to the best of my ability, and in word, at least, the requirements of the law are now satisfied. If deeds be in question, those who are here interred have received part of their honors already, and for the rest, their children will be brought up till manhood at the public expense: the state thus offers a valuable prize, as the garland of victory in this contest of valor, for the reward both of those who have fallen and their survivors. And where the rewards for merit are greatest, there are found the best citizens. And now that you have brought to a close your lamentations for your relatives, you may depart."

The Plague

47. Such was the funeral that took place during this winter, with which the first year of the war came to an end. In the first days of summer the Lacedaemonians and their allies, with two-thirds of their forces as before, invaded Attica, under the command of Archidamus, son of Zeuxidamus, King of Lacedaemon, and sat down and laid waste the country. Not many days after their arrival in Attica, the plague first began to show itself among the Athenians. It was said that it had broken out in many places previously in the neighborhood of Lemnos and elsewhere; but a pestilence of such extent and mortality was nowhere remembered. Neither were the physicians at first of any service, ignorant as they were of the proper way to treat it, but they died themselves in greatest numbers, as they visited the sick most often; nor did any human skill succeed any better. Supplications in the temples, divinations, and so forth were found equally futile, till the overwhelming nature of the disaster at last put a stop to them altogether.

48. It began, it is said, in the parts of Ethiopia above Egypt, and from there descended into Egypt and Libya and into most of the King's country. Suddenly falling upon Athens, it first attacked the population in Piraeus—which was the occasion of their saying that the Peloponnesians had poisoned the reservoirs, there being as yet no wells there—and afterwards appeared in the upper city, when the deaths became much more frequent. All speculation as to its origin and its causes, if causes can be found adequate to produce so great a disturbance, I leave to other writers, whether amateur or professional; for myself, I shall simply set down its nature, and explain the symptoms by which perhaps it may be recognized by the student, if it should ever break out again. This I can the better do, as I had the disease myself, and watched it affect others.

49. That year then is generally acknowledged to have been otherwise unprecedentedly free from sickness; and such few cases as occurred all determined in this. As a rule, however, there was no visible cause; but people in good health were suddenly attacked by violent fevers, and redness and inflammation in the eyes, the inward parts, such as the throat or tongue, becoming bloody and emitting an unnatural and fetid breath. These symptoms were followed by sneezing and hoarseness, after which the pain soon reached the chest, and produced a hard cough. When it entered the stomach, it upset it; and discharges of bile of every kind named by physicians ensued, accompanied by very great distress. In most cases also an ineffectual retching followed, producing violent spasms, which in some cases ceased soon after, in others much later. Externally the body was not very hot to the touch, nor pale in its appearance, but reddish, livid, and breaking out into small sores and ulcers. But internally it burned so that the patient could not bear to have on him clothing or even very light linen; or indeed to be otherwise than stark naked. They would have preferred to hurl themselves into cold water; as indeed was done by some of the neglected sick, who plunged into the rain-tanks in their agonies of unquenchable thirst; though it made no difference whether they drank little or much. Besides this, the miserable feeling of not being able to rest or sleep never ceased to torment them. The body meanwhile did not waste away so long as the illness was at its height, but held out to a marvel against its ravages; so that when they succumbed, as in most cases, on the seventh or eighth day to the internal inflammation, they had still some strength in them. But if they passed this stage, and the disease descended further into the bowels, inducing a violent ulceration there accompanied by severe diarrhea, this brought on a weakness which was generally fatal. For the disorder first settled in the head, ran its course from thence through the whole of the body, and, even where it did not prove fatal, it still left its mark on the extremities; for it settled in the genitals, the fingers and the toes, and many escaped with the loss of these, some too their eyes. Others again were seized with an entire loss of memory on their first recovery, and did not know either themselves or their friends.

50. But while the nature of the illness was such as to baffle all description, and its attacks almost too grievous for human nature to endure, its difference from all ordinary disorders was most clearly shown by how all the birds and beasts that prey upon human bodies, either abstained from touching them (though there were many lying unburied), or died after tasting them. In proof of this, it was noticed that birds of this kind actually disappeared; they were not around the bodies, or indeed to be seen at all. But of course the effects which I have mentioned could best be studied in a domestic animal like the dog.

51. Such then, if we pass over the varieties of particular cases which were many and peculiar, were the general features of the illness. Meanwhile the town enjoyed an immunity from all the ordinary disorders; or if any case occurred, it ended in this. Some died in neglect, others in the midst of every attention. No specific remedy was found; for what did good in one case, did harm in another. Strong and weak constitutions proved equally incapable of resistance, all alike being swept away, although treated with the utmost precaution. By far the most terrible feature in the malady was the dejection which ensued when any one felt himself sickening, for the despair into which they instantly fell took away their power of resistance, and left them a much easier prey to the disorder; besides which, there was the awful spectacle of men dying like sheep, through having caught the infection in nursing each other. This caused the greatest mortality. On the one hand, if they were afraid to visit each other, they perished from neglect; indeed many houses were emptied of their residents for want of a nurse: on the other, if they ventured to do so, death was the result. This was especially the case with those who made any pretensions to goodness: honor made them unsparing of themselves in their attendance in their friends' houses, where even the members of the family were at last worn out by the moans of the dying, and succumbed to the force of the disaster. Yet it was with those who had recovered from the disease that the sick and the dying found most compassion. These knew what it was from experience, and had now no fear for themselves; for the same man was never attacked twice—never at least fatally. And such persons not only received the congratulations of others, but themselves also, in the elation of the moment, half entertained the vain hope that they were for the future safe from any disease whatsoever.

52. An aggravation of the existing calamity was the influx from the country into the city, and this was especially felt by the new arrivals. As there were no houses to receive them, they had to be lodged in the summer in stifling cabins, where death raged without restraint. The bodies of dying men lay one upon another, and half-dead people reeled about the streets and gathered round all the fountains in their longing for water. The sacred places also in which they had quartered themselves were full of corpses of persons that had died there, just as they were; for as the disaster passed all bounds, men, not knowing what was to become of them, became utterly careless of everything, whether sacred or profane. All the burial rites before in use were entirely upset, and they buried the bodies as best they could. Many from want of the proper means, through so many of their friends having died already, had recourse to the most shameless burial methods: sometimes getting the start of those who had raised a pile, they threw their own dead body upon the stranger's pyre and ignited it; sometimes they tossed the corpse which they were carrying on the top of another that was burning, and so went off.

53. Nor was this the only form of lawless extravagance which owed its origin to the plague. Men now openly ventured on what they had formerly done in a corner, and not just as they pleased, seeing the rapid transitions produced by persons in prosperity suddenly dying and those who before had nothing succeeding to their property. So they resolved to spend quickly and enjoy themselves, regarding their lives and riches as alike things of a day. Perseverance in what men called honor was popular with none, it was so uncertain whether they would be spared to attain the object; but it was settled that present enjoyment, and all that contributed to it, was both honorable and useful. Fear of gods or law of man there was none to restrain them. As for the first, they judged it to be just the same whether they worshipped them or not, as they saw all alike perishing; and for the last, no one expected to live to be brought to trial for his offenses, but each felt that a far severer sentence had been already passed upon them all and hung ever over their heads, and before this fell it was only reasonable to enjoy life a little.

54. Such was the nature of the calamity, and heavily did it weigh on the Athenians; death raging within the city and devastation without. Among other things which they remembered in their distress was, very naturally, the following verse which the old men said had long ago been uttered:

A Dorian war shall come and with it death.

So a dispute arose as to whether dearth and not death had not been the word in the verse; but at the present juncture, it was of course decided in favor of the latter; for the people made their memory fit in with their sufferings. I fancy, however, that if another Dorian war should ever afterwards come upon us, and a dearth should happen to accompany it, the verse will probably be read accordingly. The oracle also which had been given to the Lacedaemonians was now remembered by those who knew of it. When the god was asked whether they should go to war, he answered that if they put their might into it, victory would be theirs, and that he would himself be with them. With this oracle events were supposed to tally. For the plague broke out as soon as the Peloponnesians invaded Attica, and never entering Peloponnese (not at least to an extent worth noticing), committed its worst ravages at Athens, and next to Athens, at the most populous of the other towns. Such was the history of the plague.

Evaluation of Pericles' Rule

65. Such were the arguments by which Pericles tried to cure the Athenians of their anger against him and to divert their thoughts from their immediate afflictions. As a community he succeeded in convincing them; they not only gave up all idea of sending to Lacedaemon, but applied themselves with increased energy to the war; still as private individuals they could not help smarting under their sufferings, the common people having been deprived of the little that they were possessed, while the higher orders had lost fine properties with costly establishments and buildings in the country, and, worst of all, had war instead of peace. In fact, the public feeling against him did not subside until he had been fined. Not long afterwards, however, according to the way of the multitude, they again elected him general and committed all their affairs to his hands, having now become less sensitive to their private and domestic afflictions, and understanding that he was the best man of all for the public necessities. For as long as he was at the head of the state during the peace, he pursued a moderate and conservative policy; and in his time its greatness was at its height. When the war broke out, here also he seems to have rightly gauged the power of his country. He outlived its commencement two years and six months, and the correctness of his provisions respecting it became better known by his death. He told them to wait quietly, to pay attention to their navy, to attempt no new conquests, and to expose the city to no hazards during the war, and doing this, promised them a favorable result. What they did was the very contrary, allowing private ambitions and private interests, in matters apparently quite foreign to the war, to lead them into projects unjust both to themselves and to their allies—projects whose success would only conduce to the honor and advantage of private persons, and whose failure entailed certain disaster on the country in the war. The causes of this are not far to seek. Pericles indeed, by his rank, ability, and known integrity, could exercise an independent control over the multitude in short, to lead them instead of being led by them; for as he never sought power by improper means, he was never compelled to flatter them, but, on the contrary, enjoyed so high an estimation that he could afford to anger them by contradiction. Whenever he saw them unseasonably and insolently elated, he would with a word reduce them to alarm; on the other hand, if they fell victims to a panic, he could at once restore them to confidence. In short, what was nominally a democracy became in his hands government by the first citizen. With his successors it was different. More on a level with one another, and each grasping at supremacy, they ended by committing even the conduct of state affairs to the whims of the multitude. This, as might have been expected in a great and sovereign state, produced a host of blunders, and amongst them the Sicilian expedition; though this failed not so much through a miscalculation of the power of those against whom it was sent, as through a fault in the senders in not taking the best measures afterwards to assist those who had gone out, but choosing rather to occupy themselves with private cabals for the leadership of the masses, by which they not only paralyzed operations in the field, but also first introduced civil discord at home. Yet after losing most of their fleet besides other forces in Sicily, and with faction already dominant in the city, they could still for three years make head against their original adversaries, joined not only by the Sicilians, but also by their own allies nearly all in revolt, and at last by the King's son, Cyrus, who furnished the funds for the Peloponnesian navy. Nor did they finally succumb till they fell the victims of their own internal disorders. So superfluously abundant were the resources from which the genius of Pericles foresaw an easy triumph in the war over the unaided forces of the Peloponnesians.

Edited by Marc Stier, Intellectual Heritage Program

Selections from the *Nichomachean Ethics* by Aristotle

Three works of Aristotle on ethics have survived since his time, the *Nichomachean Ethics*, the *Eudemian Ethics* and the *Magna Moralia* (although some authorities doubt that Aristotle actually wrote the third work). Three of the ten books—what we today would call chapters—of the *Nichomachean Ethics* are found among the nine books of the *Eudemian Ethics*. The doctrines of the *Nichomachean Ethics* and *Eudemian Ethics* are for the most part consistent with one another, although interpreters find some differences of greater or lesser importance between the two works. The *Nichomachean Ethics* is thought by most interpreters to be Aristotle's most mature or finished thought, although in recent years some scholars have reserved this judgment for the *Eudemian Ethics*.

The following excerpts from the *Nichomachean Ethics* have been heavily edited. I have not changed or added to the David Ross translation of the text. But I have made extensive cuts and have rearranged the various parts of the text. I have done this with some reluctance and a great deal of trepidation. I believe that, in most cases, we should never tamper with the texts of the great philosophers. The order in which philosophers present their ideas, and the structure of their books, is important. It is usually impossible to understand a philosophical text unless we pay attention to the order in which the various parts of it are put together.

I have made these changes in Aristotle's text for several reasons. First, the *Ethics* is a long and dense work, one that we cannot study as a whole in the Intellectual Heritage program. So, if we are to study the text at all, some selections must be made. Second, some features of the text make it especially difficult to study in a short time. Aristotle was a philosopher who paid close attention to both the intricacies of human life and to what previous philosophers had said about them. His views are detailed, interlinked, and comprehensive, as well as original. As a result, it is easy to get lost in Aristotle's thought. To master his ethical writings requires long study, in which one tries to put the various pieces of his thought together into a coherent whole. So, any first reading that tries to come to view of the central lines of Aristotle's thought must leave much aside, if only to avoid getting bogged down. Even a consecutive reading of the entire text is likely to focus on certain passages and leave others more or less aside. A selection of the text for first readers of it, therefore, seems necessary.

These first two reasons might justify my making some selections from the text, but by themselves they would not justify the rearrangement of parts of the text. The character of the text provides the justification for my rearrangement of the text. Aristotle's text is cryptic and compressed. Despite his detailed look at so many features of human life, many of the ideas in the *Ethics* require a great deal of elaboration. Even more, the relationship between different parts of the text is not entirely clear. Although there are some explicit transitions from one part of the text to another, at times it is not immediately clear why Aristotle moves from one topic to another. How the ideas found in the different parts of the text are meant to hang together is sometimes rather mysterious, nor are the odd repetitions easily explicable. These features of the text have led some interpreters to two conclusions about the character of the text. Some claim that the *Nichomachean Ethics* consists of lecture notes. That is, they are either the notes Aristotle used in giving his lectures in his school, the Lyceum, or they are notes prepared by Aristotle for his students, as reminders of his lectures. Other interpreters argue, following an old tradition, that the order of the text was created not by Aristotle but rather by his son Nichomachus, who brought together a variety of materials that were not necessarily written as part of a single work. That Aristotle did not bring these materials together himself is thought to be a good explanation of the awkward transitions and repetitions—as well as the curious duplication of three books in both the *Nichomachean Ethics* and the *Eudemian Ethics*. On this view, rearrangement of the text is justified, if in doing so we can improve on Nichomachus's problematic work as editor of the text.

I have some doubts about how far to take this claim. It is plausible that some features of text are due to Aristotle's never transforming his notes into a polished work or to the editorial work of others. The longer I have studied Aristotle, however, the more it appears that there are subtle reasons, having to do with the multiple audiences for the text, that account for some of the peculiarities of the structure and arrangement as well as the content, of the text.[1] If I am right about this, then an extensive study of the text should pay close attention to the structure of the text as we find it. By the same token, some rearrangement of the text might be even more necessary on an initial reading of the text. For, if Aristotle reveals some of his ideas in bits and pieces and by indirect methods, beginning readers of the text cannot hope to grasp them without a great deal of help. The main aim of my rearrangement of the text is to help readers new to Aristotle to recognize the sub-structure of his ideas about ethics, so that they can come to see why Aristotle can, with some reason, claim that moral virtue is the core of human happiness.

In what follows, the headings and my editorial comments are in *italics*. The non-italicized text is from the David Ross translation of the *Nichomachean Ethics*. The numbers in parentheses at the beginning of each paragraph give the book, chapter, and, where there is more than one, paragraph number of each selection.

Goods and Happiness

The Variety of Human Ends I: Actions and Products

(I.1) Every art and every inquiry, and similarly every action and pursuit, is thought to aim at some good; and for this reason the good has rightly been declared to be that at which all things aim. But a certain difference is found among ends; some are activities, others are products apart from the activities that produce them. Where there are ends apart from the actions, it is the nature of the products to be better than the activities. Now, as there are many actions, arts, and sciences, their ends also are many; the end of the medical art is health, that of shipbuilding a vessel, that of strategy victory, that of economics wealth. But where such arts fall under a single capacity—as bridle-making and the other arts concerned with the equipment of horses fall under the art of riding, and this and every military action under strategy, in the same way other arts fall under yet others—in all of these the ends of the master arts are to be preferred to all the subordinate ends; for it is for the sake of the former that the latter are pursued. It makes no difference whether the activities themselves are the ends of the actions, or something else apart from the activities, as in the case of the sciences just mentioned.

The Hierarchy of Goods and the Science That Studies It, Politics

(I.2) If, then, there is some end of the things we do, which we desire for its own sake (everything else being desired for the sake of this), and if we do not choose everything for the sake of something else (for at that rate the process would go on to infinity, so that our desire would be empty and vain), clearly this must be the good and the chief good. Will not the knowledge of it, then, have a great influence on life? Shall we not, like archers who have a mark to aim at, be more likely to hit upon what is right? If so, we must try, in outline at least, to determine what it is, and of which of the sciences or capacities it is the object. It would seem to belong to the most authoritative art and that which is most truly the master art. And politics appears to be of this nature; for it is this that ordains which of the sciences should be studied in a state, and which each class of citizens should learn and up to what point they should learn them; and we see even the most highly esteemed of capacities to fall under this, e.g. strategy, economics, rhetoric; now, since politics uses the rest of the sciences, and since, again, it legislates as to what we are to do and what we are to abstain from, the end of this science must include those of the others, so that this end must be the good for man. For even if the end is the same for a single man and for a state, that of the polis seems at all events something greater and more complete whether to attain or to preserve; though it is worth while to attain the end merely for one man, it is finer and more godlike to attain it for a people or for the polis. These, then, are the ends at which our inquiry aims, since it is political science, in one sense of that term.

The Hierarchy of Ends

(I.7.1) Let us again return to the good we are seeking, and ask what it can be. It seems different in different actions and arts; it is different in medicine, in strategy, and in the other arts likewise. What then is the good of each? Surely that for whose sake everything else is done. In medicine this is health, in strategy victory, in architecture a house, in any other sphere something else, and in every action and pursuit the end; for it is for the sake of this that all men do whatever else they do. Therefore, if there is an end for all that we do, this will be the good achievable by action, and if there are more than one, these will be the goods achievable by action.

(I.7.2) So the argument has by a different course reached the same point; but we must try to state this even more clearly. Since there is evidently more than one end, and we choose some of these (e.g. wealth, flutes, and in general instruments) for the sake of something else, clearly not all ends are final ends; but the chief good is evidently something final. Therefore, if there is only one final end, this will be what we are seeking, and if there are more than one, the most final of these will be what we are seeking. Now we call that which is in itself worthy of pursuit more final than that which is worthy of pursuit for the sake of something else, and that which is never desirable for the sake of something else more final than the things that are desirable both in themselves and for the sake of that other thing, and therefore we call final without qualification that which is always desirable in itself and never for the sake of something else.

Eudamonia/Happiness as the End of Human Beings

(I.7.3) Now such a thing happiness, above all else, is held to be; for this we choose always for self and never for the sake of something else, but honour, pleasure, reason, and every virtue we choose indeed for themselves (for if nothing resulted from them we should still choose each of them), but we choose them also for the sake of happiness, judging that by means of them we shall be happy. Happiness, on the other hand, no one chooses for the sake of these, nor, in general, for anything other than itself.

What Is Eudamonia? Some Possibilities

(I.4) Let us resume our inquiry and state, in view of the fact that all knowledge and every pursuit aims at some good, what it is that we say political science aims at and what is the highest of all goods achievable by action. Verbally there is very general agreement; for both the general run of men and people of superior refinement say that it is happiness, and identify living well and doing well with being happy; but with regard to what happiness is they differ, and the many do not give the same account as the wise. For the former think it is some plain and obvious thing, like pleasure, wealth, or honor; they differ, however, from one another—and often even the same man identifies it with different things, with health when he is ill, with wealth when he is poor; but, conscious of their ignorance, they admire those who proclaim some great ideal that is above their comprehension. Now some thought that apart from these many goods there is another which is self-subsistent and causes the goodness of all these as well. To examine all the opinions that have been held were perhaps somewhat fruitless; enough to examine those that are most prevalent or that seem to be arguable.

(I.5.1) Let us, however, resume our discussion from the point at which we digressed. To judge from the lives that men lead, most men, and men of the most vulgar type, seem (not without some ground) to identify the good, or happiness, with pleasure; which is the reason why they love the life of enjoyment. For there are, we may say, three prominent types of life—that just mentioned, the political, and thirdly the contemplative life. Now the mass of mankind are evidently quite slavish in their tastes, preferring a life suitable to beasts, but they get some ground for their view from the fact that many of those in high places share the tastes of Sardanapallus. A consideration of the prominent types of life shows that people of superior refinement and of active disposition identify happiness with honour; for this is, roughly speaking, the end of the political life. But it seems too superficial to be what we are looking for, since it is thought to depend on those who bestow honour rather than on him who receives it, but the good we divine to be something proper to a man and not easily taken from him. Further, men seem to pursue honour in order that they may be assured of their goodness; at least it is by men of practical wisdom that they seek to be honored, and among those who know them, and on the ground of their virtue; clearly, then, according to them, at any rate, virtue is better. And perhaps one might even suppose this to be, rather than honour, the end of the political life. But even this appears somewhat incomplete; for possession of virtue seems actually compatible with being asleep, or with lifelong inactivity, and, further, with the greatest sufferings and misfortunes; but a man who was living so no one would call happy, unless he were maintaining a thesis at all costs. But enough of this; for the subject has been sufficiently treated even in the current discussions. Third comes the contemplative life, which we shall consider later.

(I.5.2) The life of money-making is one undertaken under compulsion, and wealth is evidently not the good we are seeking; for it is merely useful and for the sake of something else. And so one might rather take the aforenamed objects to be ends; for they are loved for themselves. But it is evident that not even these are ends; yet many arguments have been thrown away in support of them. Let us leave this subject, then.

Happiness and Virtue: The Function of Man

(I.7.5) Presumably, however, to say that happiness is the chief good seems a platitude, and a clearer account of what it is still desired. This might perhaps be given, if we could first ascertain the function of man. For just as for a flute-player, a sculptor, or an artist, and, in general, for all things that have a function or activity, the good and the 'well' is thought to reside in the function, so would it seem to be for man, if he has a function. Have the carpenter, then, and the tanner certain functions or activities, and has man none? Is he born without a function? Or as eye, hand, foot, and in general each of the parts evidently has a function, may one lay it down that man similarly has a function apart from all these? What then can this be? Life seems to be common even to plants, but we are seeking what is peculiar to man. Let us exclude, therefore, the life of nutrition and growth. Next there would be a life of perception, but it also seems to be common even to the horse, the ox, and every animal. There remains, then, an active life of the element that has a rational principle; of this, one part has such a principle in the sense of being obedient to one, the other in the sense of possessing one and exercising thought. And, as 'life of the rational element' also has two meanings, we must state that life in the sense of activity is what we mean; for this seems to be the more proper sense of the term. Now if the function of man is an activity of soul which follows or implies a rational principle, and if we say 'so-and-so' and 'a good so-and-so' have a function that is the same in kind, e.g. a lyre, and a good lyre-player, and so without qualification in all cases, eminence in respect of goodness being added to the name of the function (for the function of a lyre-player is to play the lyre, and that of a good lyre-player is to do so well): if this is the case, and we state the function of man to be a certain kind of life, and this to be an activity or actions of the soul implying a rational principle, and the function of a good man to be the good and noble performance of these, and if any action is well performed when it is performed in accordance with the appropriate excellence: if this is the case, human good turns out to be activity of soul in accordance with virtue, and if there are more than one virtue, in accordance with the best and most complete.

(I.7.6) But we must add 'in a complete life.' For one swallow does not make a summer, nor does one day; and so too one day, or a short time, does not make a man blessed and happy.

The Variety of Human Ends II: Internal and External Goods

(I.8.1) We must consider it, however, in the light not only of our conclusion and our premises, but also of what is commonly said about it; for with a true view all the data harmonize, but with a false one the facts soon clash. Now goods have been divided into three classes, and some are described as external, others as relating to soul or to body; we call those that relate to soul most properly and truly goods, and psychical actions and activities we class as relating to soul. Therefore our account must be sound, at least according to this view, which is an old one and agreed on by philosophers. It is correct also in that we identify the end with certain actions and activities; for thus it falls among goods of the soul and not among external goods. Another belief that harmonizes with our account is that the happy man lives well and does well; for we have practically defined happiness as a sort of good life and good action. The characteristics that are looked for in happiness seem also, all of them, to belong to what we have defined happiness as being. For some identify happiness with virtue, some with practical wisdom, others with a kind of philosophic wisdom, others with these, or one of these, accompanied by pleasure or not without pleasure; while others include also external prosperity. Now some of these views have been held by many men and men of old, others by a few eminent persons; and it is not probable that either of these should be entirely mistaken, but rather that they should be right in at least some one respect or even in most respects.

(I.8.2) With those who identify happiness with virtue or some one virtue our account is in harmony; for to virtue belongs virtuous activity. But it makes, perhaps, no small difference whether we place the chief good in possession or in use, in state of mind or in activity. For the state of mind may exist without producing any good result, as in a man who is asleep or in some other way quite inactive, but the activity cannot; for one who has the activity will of necessity be acting, and acting well. And as in the Olympic Games it is not the most beautiful and the strongest that are crowned but those who compete (for it is some of these that are victorious), so those who act win, and rightly win, the noble and good things in life.

(I.8.3) Their life is also in itself pleasant. For pleasure is a state of soul, and to each man that which he is said to be a lover of is pleasant; e.g. not only is a horse pleasant to the lover of horses, and a spectacle to the lover of sights, but also in the same way just acts are pleasant to the lover of justice and in general virtuous acts to the lover of virtue. Now for most men their pleasures are in conflict with one another because these are not by nature pleasant, but the lovers of what is noble find pleasant the things that are by nature pleasant; and virtuous actions are such, so that these are pleasant for such men as well as in their own nature. Their life, therefore, has no further need of pleasure as a sort of adventitious charm, but has its pleasure in itself. For, besides what we have said, the man who does not rejoice in noble actions is not even good; since no one would call a man just who did not enjoy acting justly, nor any man liberal who did not enjoy liberal actions; and similarly in all other cases. If this is so, virtuous actions must be in themselves pleasant. But they are also good and noble, and have each of these attributes in the highest degree, since the good man judges well about these attributes; his judgment is such as we have described. Happiness then is the best, noblest, and most pleasant thing in the world, and these attributes are not severed as in the inscription at Delos—

> Most noble is that which is justest, and best is health;
> But pleasantest is it to win what we love.
> For all these properties belong to the best activities; and these, or one
> the best—of these, we identify with happiness.

(I.8.4) Yet evidently, as we said, it needs the external goods as well; for it is impossible, or not easy, to do noble acts without the proper equipment. In many actions we use friends and riches and political power as instruments; and there are some things the lack of which takes the luster from happiness, as good birth, goodly children, beauty; for the man who is very ugly in appearance or ill-born or solitary and childless is not very likely to be happy, and perhaps a man would be still less likely if he had thoroughly bad children or friends or had lost good children or friends by death. As we said, then, happiness seems to need this sort of prosperity in addition; for which reason some identify happiness with good fortune, though others identify it with virtue.

Eudamonia and Self-Sufficiency/Luck and Fortune

(I.7.4) From the point of view of self-sufficiency the same result seems to follow; for the final good is thought to be self-sufficient. Now by self-sufficient we do not mean that which is sufficient for a man by himself, for one who lives a solitary life, but also for parents, children, wife, and in general for his friends and fellow citizens, since man is born for citizenship. But some limit must be set to this; for if we extend our requirement to ancestors and descendants and friends' friends we are in for an infinite series. Let us examine this question, however, on another occasion; the self-sufficient we now define as that which when isolated makes life desirable and lacking in nothing; and such we think happiness to be; and further we think it most desirable of all things, without being counted as one good thing among others—if it were so counted it would clearly be made more desirable by the addition of even the least of goods; for that which is added becomes an excess of goods, and of goods the greater is always more desirable. Happiness, then, is something final and self-sufficient, and is the end of action.

(I.9.1) For this reason also the question is asked, whether happiness is to be acquired by learning or by habituation or some other sort of training, or comes in virtue of some divine providence or again by chance. Now if there is any gift of the gods to men, it is reasonable that happiness should be god-given, and most surely god-given of all human things inasmuch as it is the best. But this question would perhaps be more appropriate to another inquiry; happiness seems, however, even if it is not god-sent but comes as a result of virtue and some process of learning or training, to be among the most godlike things; for that which is the prize and end of virtue seems to be the best thing in the world, and something godlike and blessed.

(I.9.2) It will also on this view be very generally shared; for all who are not maimed as regards their potentiality for virtue may win it by a certain kind of study and care. But if it is better to be happy thus than by chance, it is reasonable that the facts should be so, since everything that depends on the action of nature is by nature as good as it can be, and similarly everything that depends on art or any rational cause, and especially if it depends on the best of all causes. To entrust to chance what is greatest and most noble would be a very defective arrangement.

(I.9.3) The answer to the question we are asking is plain also from the definition of happiness; for it has been said to be a virtuous activity of soul, of a certain kind. Of the remaining goods, some must necessarily pre-exist as conditions of happiness, and others are naturally co-operative and useful as instruments. And this will be found to agree with what we said at the outset; for we stated the end of political science to be the best end, and political science spends most of its pains on making the citizens to be of a certain character, namely, good and capable of noble acts.

(I.9.4) It is natural, then, that we call neither ox nor horse nor any other of the animals happy; for none of them is capable of sharing in such activity. . . . For there is required, as we said, not only complete virtue but also a complete life, since many changes occur in life, and all manner of chances, and the most prosperous may fall into great misfortunes in old age, as is told of Priam in the Trojan Cycle; and one who has experienced such chances and has ended wretchedly no one calls happy.

(I.10.2) But we must return to our first difficulty; for perhaps by a consideration of it our present problem might be solved. Now if we must see the end (*of a man's life*) and only then call a man happy, not as being happy but as having been so before, surely this is a paradox, that when he is happy the attribute that belongs to him is not to be truly predicated of him because we do not wish to call living men happy, on account of the changes that may befall them, and because we have assumed happiness to be something permanent and by no means easily changed, while a single man may suffer many turns of fortune's wheel. For clearly if we were to keep pace with his fortunes, we should often call the same man happy and again wretched, making the happy man out to be chameleon and insecurely based. Or is this keeping pace with his fortunes quite wrong? Success or failure in life does not depend on these, but human life, as we said, needs these as mere additions, while virtuous activities or their opposites are what constitute happiness or the reverse.

(I.10.3) The question we have now discussed confirms our definition. For no function of man has so much permanence as virtuous activities (these are thought to be more durable even than knowledge of the sciences), and of these themselves the most valuable are more durable because those who are happy spend their life most readily and most continuously in these; for this seems to be the reason why we do not forget them. The attribute in question, then, will belong to the happy man, and he will be happy throughout his life; for always, or by preference to everything else, he will be engaged in virtuous action and contemplation, and he will bear the chances of life most nobly and altogether decorously, if he is 'truly good' and 'foursquare beyond reproach'.

(I.10.4) Now many events happen by chance, and events differing in importance; small pieces of good fortune or of its opposite clearly do not weigh down the scales of life one way or the other, but a multitude of great events if they turn out well will make life happier (for not only are they themselves such as to add beauty to life, but the way a man deals with them may be noble and good), while if they turn out ill they crush and maim happiness; for they both bring pain with them and hinder many activities. Yet even in these nobility shines through, when a man bears with resignation many great misfortunes, not through insensibility to pain but through nobility and greatness of soul.

(I.10.5) If activities are, as we said, what gives life its character, no happy man can become miserable; for he will never do the acts that are hateful and mean. For the man who is truly good and wise, we think, bears all the chances life becomingly and always makes the best of circumstances, as a good general makes the best military use of the army at his command and a good shoemaker makes the best shoes out of the hides that are given him; and so with all other craftsmen. And if this is the case, the happy man can never become miserable; though he will not reach blessedness, if he meet with fortunes like those of Priam.

(I.10.6) Nor, again, is he many-coloured and changeable; for neither will he be moved from his happy state easily or by any ordinary misadventures, but only by many great ones, nor, if he has had many great misadventures, will he recover his happiness in a short time, but if at all, only in a long and complete one in which he has attained many splendid successes.

(I.10.7) When then should we not say that he is happy who is active in accordance with complete virtue and is sufficiently equipped with external goods, not for some chance period but throughout a complete life? Or must we add 'and who is destined to live thus and die as befits his life'? Certainly the future is obscure to us, while happiness, we claim, is an end and something in every way final. If so, we shall call happy those among living men in whom these conditions are, and are to be, fulfilled—but happy men. So much for these questions.

The Nature of the Study of Ethics

(I.3.1) Our discussion will be adequate if it has as much clearness as the subject-matter admits of, for precision is not to be sought for alike in all discussions, any more than in all the products of the crafts. Now fine and just actions, which political science investigates, admit of much variety and fluctuation of opinion, so that they may be thought to exist only by convention, and not by nature. And goods also give rise to a similar fluctuation because they bring harm to many people; for before now men have been undone by reason of their wealth, and others by reason of their courage. We must be content, then, in speaking of such subjects and with such premises to indicate the truth roughly and in outline, and in speaking about things that are only for the most part true and with premises of the same kind to reach conclusions that are no better. In the same spirit, therefore, should each type of statement be received; for it is the mark of an educated man to look for precision in each class of things just so far as the nature of the subject admits; it is evidently equally foolish to accept probable reasoning from a mathematician and to demand from a rhetorician scientific proofs.

(I.3.2) Now each man judges well the things he knows, and of these he is a good judge. And so the man who has been educated in a subject is a good judge of that subject, and the man who has received an all-around education is a good judge in general. Hence a young man is not a proper hearer of lectures on political science; for he is inexperienced in the actions that occur in life, but its discussions start from these and are about these; and, further, since he tends to follow his passions, his study will be vain and unprofitable, because the end aimed at is not knowledge but action. And it makes no difference whether he is young in years or youthful in character; the defect does not depend on time, but on his living, and pursuing each successive object, as passion directs. For to such persons, as to the incontinent, knowledge brings no profit; but to those who desire and act in accordance with a rational principle knowledge about such matters will be of great benefit.

(I.4) Let us not fail to notice, however, that there is a difference between arguments from and those to the first principles. For Plato, too, was right in raising this question and asking, as he used to do, 'are we on the way from or to the first principles?' There is a difference, as there is in a race-course between the course from the judges to the turning-point and the way back. For, while we must begin with what is known, things are objects of knowledge in two senses—some to us, some without qualification. Presumably, then, we must begin with things known to us. Hence any one who is to listen intelligently to lectures about what is noble and just, and generally, about the subjects of political science must have been brought up in good habits. For the fact is the starting point, and if this is sufficiently plain to him, he will not at the start need the reason as well; and the man who has been well brought up has or can easily get starting points. And as for him who neither has nor can get them, let him hear the words of Hesiod:

> Far best is he who knows all things himself;
> Good, he that hearkens when men counsel right;
> But he who neither knows, nor lays to heart
> Another's wisdom, is a useless weight.

The Soul

Parts of the Soul

(I.13.1) Since happiness is an activity of soul in accordance with perfect virtue, we must consider the nature of virtue; for perhaps we shall thus see better the nature of happiness. The true student of politics, too, is thought to have studied virtue above all things; for he wishes to make his fellow citizens good and obedient to the laws. . . . But clearly the virtue we must study is human virtue; for the good we were seeking was human good and the happiness human happiness. By human virtue we mean not that of the body but that of the soul; and happiness also we call an activity of soul. But if this is so, clearly the student of politics must know somehow the facts about soul, as the man who is to heal the eyes or the body as a whole must know about the eyes or the body; and all the more since politics is more prized and better than medicine; but even among doctors the best educated spend much labor on acquiring knowledge of the body.

(I.13.2) Some things are said about it, adequately enough, even in the discussions outside our school, and we must use these; e.g. that one element in the soul is irrational and one has a rational principle.

(I.13.3) Of the irrational element one division seems to be widely distributed, and vegetative in its nature, I mean that which causes nutrition and growth; for it is this kind of power of the soul that one must assign to all nurslings and to embryos, and this same power to full grown creatures; this is more reasonable than to assign some different power to them. Now the excellence of this seems to be common to all species and not specifically human . . . let us leave the nutritive faculty alone, since it has by its nature no share in human excellence.

(I.13.4) There seems to be also another irrational element in the soul—one which in a sense, however, shares in a rational principle. For we praise the rational principle of the continent man and of the incontinent, and the part of their soul that has such a principle, since it urges them aright and towards the best objects; but there is found in them also another element naturally opposed to the rational principle, which fights against and resists that principle. For exactly as paralyzed limbs when we intend to move them to the right turn on the contrary to the left, so is it with the soul; the impulses of incontinent people move in contrary directions. But while in the body we see that which moves astray, in the soul we do not. No doubt, however, we must none the less suppose that in the soul too there is something contrary to the rational principle, resisting and opposing it. In what sense it is distinct from the other elements does not concern us. Now even this seems to have a share in a rational principle, as we said; at any rate in the continent man it obeys the rational principle and presumably in the temperate and brave man it is still more obedient; for in him it speaks, on all matters, with the same voice as the rational principle.

(I.13.5) Therefore the irrational element also appears to be twofold. For the vegetative element in no way shares in a rational principle, but the appetitive and in general the desiring element in a sense shares in it, in so far as it listens to and obeys. ... That the irrational element is in some sense persuaded by a rational principle is indicated also by the giving of advice and by all reproof and exhortation. And if this element also must be said to have a rational principle, that which has a rational principle (as well as that which has not) will be twofold, one subdivision having it in the strict sense and in itself, and the other having a tendency to obey as one does one's father.

(I.13.6) Virtue too is distinguished into kinds in accordance with this difference; for we say that some of the virtues are intellectual and others moral, philosophic wisdom and understanding and practical wisdom being intellectual, liberality and temperance moral. For in speaking about a man's character we do not say that he is wise or has understanding but that he is good-tempered or temperate; yet we praise the wise man also with respect to his state of mind; and of states of mind we call those that merit praise virtues.

The Nature of Moral Virtue

Moral Virtue and Habituation

(II.1.1) Virtue, then, being of two kinds, intellectual and moral, intellectual virtue in the main owes both its birth and its growth to teaching (for which reason it requires experience and time), while moral virtue comes about as a result of habit, whence also its name (*ethike*) is one that is formed by a slight variation from the word *ethos* (habit). From this it is also plain that none of the moral virtues arises in us by nature; for nothing that exists by nature can form a habit contrary to its nature.

(II.1.2) Again, of all the things that come to us by nature we first acquire the potentiality and later exhibit the activity (this is plain in the case of the senses; for it was not by often seeing or often hearing that we got these senses, but on the contrary we had them before we used them, and did not come to have them by using them); but the virtues we get by first exercising them, as also happens in the case of the arts as well. For the things we have to learn before we can do them, we learn by doing them, e.g. men become builders by building and lyre-players by playing the lyre; so too we become just by doing just acts, temperate by doing temperate acts, brave by doing brave acts.

(II.1.3) This is confirmed by what happens in states; for legislators make the citizens good by forming habits in them, and this is the wish of every legislator, and those who do not effect it miss their mark, and it is in this that a good constitution differs from a bad one.

(II.1.4) Again, it is from the same causes and by the same means that every virtue is both produced and destroyed, and similarly every art; for it is from playing the lyre that both good and bad lyre-players are produced. And the corresponding statement is true of builders and of all the rest; men will be good or bad builders as a result of building well or badly. For if this were not so, there would have been no need of a teacher, but all men would have been born good or bad at their craft. This, then, is the case with the virtues also; by doing the acts that we do in our transactions with other men we become just or unjust, and by doing the acts that we do in the presence of danger, and being habituated to feel fear or confidence, we become brave or cowardly. The same is true of appetites and feelings of anger; some men become temperate and good-tempered, others self-indulgent and irascible, by behaving in one way or the other in the appropriate circumstances.

(II.2.1) Since, then, the present inquiry does not aim at theoretical knowledge like the others (for we are inquiring not in order to know what virtue is, but in order to become good, since otherwise our inquiry would have been of no use), we must examine the nature of actions, namely how we ought to do them; for these determine also the nature of the states of character that are produced, as we have said.

We Become Virtuous by Doing Virtuous Actions: Further Considerations

(II.4.1) The question might be asked; what we mean by saying that we must become just by doing just acts, and temperate by doing temperate acts; for if men do just and temperate acts, they are already just and temperate, exactly as, if they do what is in accordance with the laws of grammar and of music, they are grammarians and musicians.

(II.4.3) . . . if the acts that are in accordance with the virtues have themselves a certain character it does not follow that they are done justly or temperately. The agent also must be in a certain condition when he does them; in the first place he must have knowledge, secondly he must choose the acts, and choose them for their own sakes, and thirdly his action must proceed from a firm and unchangeable character.

(II.4.4) Actions, then, are called just and temperate when they are such as the just or the temperate man would do; but it is not the man who does these that is just and temperate, but the man who also does them as just and temperate men do them. It is well said, then, that it is by doing just acts that the just man is produced, and by doing temperate acts the temperate man; without doing these no one would have even a prospect of becoming good.

(II.4.5) But most people do not do these, but take refuge in theory and think they are being philosophers and will become good in this way, behaving somewhat like patients who listen attentively to their doctors, but do none of the things they are ordered to do. As the latter will not be made well in body by such a course of treatment, the former will not be made well in soul by such a course of philosophy.

Virtues and States of Character

(II.5.1) Next we must consider what virtue is. Since things that are found in the soul are of three kinds—passions, faculties, states of character—virtue must be one of these. By passions I mean appetite, anger, fear, confidence, envy, joy, friendly feeling, hatred, longing, emulation, pity, and in general the feelings that are accompanied by pleasure or pain; by faculties the things in virtue of which we are said to be capable of feeling these, e.g. of becoming angry or being pained or feeling pity; by states of character the things in virtue of which we stand well or badly with reference to the passions, e.g. with reference to anger we stand badly if we feel it violently or too weakly, and well if we feel it moderately; and similarly with reference to the other passions.

(II.5.2) Now neither the virtues nor the vices are passions, because we are not called good or bad on the ground of our passions, but are so called on the ground of our virtues and our vices, and because we are neither praised nor blamed for our passions (for the man who feels fear or anger is not praised, nor is the man who simply feels anger blamed, but the man who feels it in a certain way), but for our virtues and our vices we are praised or blamed.

(II.5.3) Again, we feel anger and fear without choice, but the virtues are modes of choice or involve choice. Further, in respect of the passions we are said to be moved, but in respect of the virtues and the vices we are said not to be moved but to be disposed in a particular way.

(II.5.4) For these reasons also they are not faculties; for we are neither called good nor bad, nor praised nor blamed, for the simple capacity of feeling the passions; again, we have the faculties by nature, but we are not made good or bad by nature; we have spoken of this before. If, then, the virtues are neither passions nor faculties, all that remains is that they should be states of character.

(II.5.5) Thus we have stated what virtue is in respect of its genus.

(II.6.1) We must, however, not only describe virtue as a state of character, but also say what sort of state it is. We may remark, then, that every virtue or excellence both brings into good condition the thing of which it is the excellence and makes the work of that thing be done well; e.g. the excellence of the eye makes both the eye and its work good; for it is by the excellence of the eye that we see well. Similarly the excellence of the horse makes a horse both good in itself and good at running and at carrying its rider and at awaiting the attack of the enemy. Therefore, if this is true in every case, the virtue of man also will be the state of character which makes a man good and which makes him do his own work well.

Virtues Aim at the Mean Relative to Us

(II.2.2) But though our present account is of this nature we must give what help we can. First, then, let us consider this, that it is the nature of such things to be destroyed by defect and excess, as we see in the case of strength and of health (for to gain light on things imperceptible we must use the evidence of sensible things); both excessive and defective exercise destroys the strength, and similarly drink or food that is above or below a certain amount destroys the health, while that which is proportionate both produces and increases and preserves it. So too is it, then, in the case of temperance and courage and the other virtues. For the man who flies from and fears everything and does not stand his ground against anything becomes a coward, and the man who fears nothing at all but goes to meet every danger becomes rash; and similarly the man who indulges in every pleasure and abstains from none becomes self-indulgent, while the man who shuns every pleasure, as boors do, becomes in a way insensible; temperance and courage, then, are destroyed by excess and defect, and preserved by the mean.

(II.3.1) We must take as a sign of states of character the pleasure or pain that ensues on acts; for the man who abstains from bodily pleasures and delights in this very fact is temperate, while the man who is annoyed at it is self-indulgent, and he who stands his ground against things that are terrible and delights in this or at least is not pained is brave, while the man who is pained is a coward. For moral excellence is concerned with pleasures and pains; it is on account of the pleasure that we do bad things, and on account of the pain that we abstain from noble ones. Hence we ought to have been brought up in a particular way from our very youth, as Plato says, so as both to delight in and to be pained by the things that we ought; for this is the right education.

(II.6.2) How this is to happen we have stated already, but it will be made plain also by the following consideration of the specific nature of virtue. In everything that is continuous and divisible it is possible to take more, less, or an equal amount, and that either in terms of the thing itself or relatively to us; and the equal is an intermediate between excess and defect. By the intermediate in the object I mean that which is equidistant from each of the extremes, which is one and the same for all men; by the intermediate relatively to us that which is neither too much nor too little—and this is not one, nor the same for all. For instance, if ten is many and two is few, six is the intermediate, taken in terms of the object; for it exceeds and is exceeded by an equal amount; this is intermediate according to arithmetical proportion. But the intermediate relatively to us is not to be taken so; if ten pounds are too much for a particular person to eat and two too little, it does not follow that the trainer will order six pounds; for this also is perhaps too much for the person who is to take it, or too little—too little for Milo, too much for the beginner in athletic exercises. The same is true of running and wrestling. Thus a master of any art avoids excess and defect, but seeks the intermediate and chooses this—the intermediate not in the object but relatively to us.

(II.6.3) ... virtue must have the quality of aiming at the intermediate. I mean moral virtue; for it is this that is concerned with passions and actions, and in these there is excess, defect, and the intermediate. For instance, both fear and confidence and appetite and anger and pity and in general pleasure and pain may be felt both too much and too little, and in both cases not well; but to feel them at the right times, with reference to the right objects, towards the right people, with the right motive, and in the right way, is what is both intermediate and best, and this is characteristic of virtue. Similarly with regard to actions also there is excess, defect, and the intermediate. Now virtue is concerned with passions and actions, in which excess is a form of failure, and so is defect, while the intermediate is praised and is a form of success; and being praised and being successful are both characteristics of virtue. Therefore virtue is a kind of mean, since, as we have seen, it aims at what is intermediate.

(II.6.5) Virtue, then, is a state of character concerned with choice, lying in a mean, i.e. the mean relative to us, this being determined by a rational principle, and by that principle by which the man of practical wisdom would determine it. Now it is a mean between two vices, that which depends on excess and that which depends on defect; and again it is a mean because the vices respectively fall short of or exceed what is right in both passions and actions, while virtue both finds and chooses that which is intermediate. Hence in respect of its substance and the definition which states its essence virtue is a mean, with regard to what is best and right an extreme.

An Outline of the Virtues

Overview of the Virtues

(II.7.1) We must, however, not only make this general statement, but also apply it to the individual facts. For among statements about conduct, those that are general apply more widely, but those that are particular are more genuine, since conduct has to do with individual cases, and our statements must harmonize with the facts in these cases. We may take these cases from our table. With regard to feelings of fear and confidence, courage is the mean; of the people who exceed, he who exceeds in fearlessness has no name (many of the states have no name), while the man who exceeds in confidence is rash, and he who exceeds in fear and falls short in confidence is a coward. With regard to pleasures and pains—not all of them, and not so much with regard to the pains—the mean is temperance, the excess self-indulgence. Persons deficient with regard to the pleasures are not often found; hence such persons also have received no name. But let us call them 'insensible'.

(II.7.2) With regard to giving and taking of money the mean is liberality, the excess and the defect prodigality and meanness. In these actions, people exceed and fall short in contrary ways; the prodigal exceeds in spending and falls short in taking, while the mean man exceeds in taking and falls short in spending. (At present we are giving a mere outline or summary, and are satisfied with this; later these states will be more exactly determined.) With regard to money there are also other dispositions—a mean, magnificence (for the magnificent man differs from the liberal man; the former deals with large sums, the latter with small ones), an excess, tastelessness and vulgarity, and a deficiency, stinginess; these differ from the states opposed to liberality, and the mode of their difference will be stated later. With regard to honor and dishonor the mean is proper pride, the excess is known as a sort of 'empty vanity', and the deficiency is undue humility; and as we said liberality was related to magnificence, differing from it by dealing with small sums, so there is a state similarly related to proper pride, being concerned with small honours while that is concerned with great. For it is possible to desire honour as one ought, and more than one ought, and less, and the man who exceeds in his desires is called ambitious, the man who falls short unambitious, while the intermediate person has no name. The dispositions also are nameless, except that that of the ambitious man is called ambition. Hence the people who are at the extremes lay claim to the middle place; and we ourselves sometimes call the intermediate person ambitious and sometimes unambitious, and sometimes praise the ambitious man and sometimes the unambitious. The reason of our doing this will be stated in what follows; but now let us speak of the remaining states according to the method that has been indicated.

(II.7.3) With regard to anger also there is an excess, a deficiency, and a mean. Although they can scarcely be said to have names, yet since we call the intermediate person good-tempered let us call the mean good temper; of the persons at the extremes let the one who exceeds be called irascible, and his vice irascibility, and the man who falls short an inirascible sort of person, and the deficiency inirascibility.

(II.7.4) There are also three other means, which have a certain likeness to one another, but differ from one another: for they are all concerned with intercourse in words and actions, but differ in that one is concerned with truth in this sphere, the other two with pleasantness; and of this one kind is exhibited in giving amusement, the other in all the circumstances of life. We must therefore speak of these too, that we may the better see that in all things the mean is praiseworthy, and the extremes neither praiseworthy nor right, but worthy of blame. Now most of these states also have no names, but we must try, as in the other cases, to invent names ourselves so that we may be clear and easy to follow. With regard to truth, then, the intermediate is a truthful sort of person and the mean may be called truthfulness, while the pretence that exaggerates is boastfulness and the person characterized by it a boaster, and that which understates is mock modesty and the person characterized by it mockmodest. With regard to pleasantness in the giving of amusement, the intermediate person is ready-witted and the disposition ready wit, the excess is buffoonery and the person characterized by it a buffoon, while the man who falls short is a sort of boor and his state is boorishness. With regard to the remaining kind of pleasantness, that which is exhibited in life in general, the man who is pleasant in the right way is friendly and the mean is friendliness, while the man who exceeds is an obsequious person if he has no end in view, a flatterer if he is aiming at his own advantage, and the man who falls short and is unpleasant in all circumstances is a quarrelsome and surly sort of person.

(II.7.5) There are also means in the passions and concerned with the passions; since shame is not a virtue, and yet praise is extended to the modest man. For even in these matters one man is said to be intermediate, and another to exceed, as for instance the bashful man who is ashamed of everything; while he who falls short or is not ashamed of anything at all is shameless, and the intermediate person is modest. Righteous indignation is a mean between envy and spite, and these states are concerned with the pain and pleasure that are felt at the fortunes of our neighbours; the man who is characterized by righteous indignation is pained at undeserved good fortune; the envious man, going beyond him, is pained at all good fortune, and the spiteful man falls so far short of being pained that he even rejoices. But these states there will be an opportunity of describing elsewhere; with regard to justice, since it has not one simple meaning, we shall, after describing the other states, distinguish its two kinds and say how each of them is a mean; and similarly we shall treat also of the rational virtues.

A List of the Virtues with Common English Translations

Editor's Note: In the following chart, the virtue is in the second column, first in the English translation given it by Ross and then after a slash in the English translation by Irwin where it differs. I have also put in parentheses other English translations of the Greek terms for the virtues and vices found in other translations of Plato and Aristotle. The two vices associated with each virtue are found in the first and third columns. In some cases, there is more than one vice, because a person can

Vice of Deficiency	Virtue	Vice of Excess	Comments
Cowardly	Courageous/Brave	Excessively fearless, Excessively confident or Rashness	Feelings of fear and confidence
Insensibile	Temperate (Moderate)	Self-indulgent/ Intemperate	Pleasure and pain, particularly bodily pleasures
Mean/Ungenerous	Liberal/Generous	Prodigal/Wasteful	Money
Stingy	Magnificent	Tasteless and Vulgar/Ostentatious and Vulgar	Money, with regard to large expenditures
Unduly humble/ Pusillanimous	Properly prideful/ Magnanimous	Vain	Honor, with regard to large honors
Unambitious/ Indifferent to honor		Ambitious/ Honor-loving	Honor, with regard to small honors
Inirascible	Good-tempered/ Mild	Irascible	Anger
Mock modest/ Self-deprecating	Truthful	Boastful	Honesty
Boorish	Ready-witted	Buffoonery	Pleasantness in the giving of amusement
Quarrelsome, Surly/Quarrelsome, Ill-tempered	Friendly	Obsequious, Flatterer/ Ingratiating, Flatterer	Pleasantness in general
	Just (in general sense)		
	Just (in particular sense)		

lack a particular virtue in more than one way. Note that some of the virtues and vices have no names. The fourth column contains some comments about the nature of the virtue.

Pleasure

The Importance of Studying Pleasure

(VII.11.1) The study of pleasure and pain belongs to the province of the political philosopher; for he is the architect of the end, with a view to which we call one thing bad and another good without qualification. Further, it is one of our necessary tasks to consider them; for not only did we lay it down that moral virtue and vice are concerned with pains and pleasures, but most people say that happiness involves pleasure; this is why the blessed man is called by a name derived from a word meaning "enjoyment."

Types of Pleasures I: Restoring Our Natural State

(VII.12.2) Further, one kind of good being activity and another being state, the processes that restore us to our natural state are only incidentally pleasant; for that matter the activity at work in the appetites for them is the activity of so much of our state and nature as has remained unimpaired; for there are actually pleasures that involve no pain or appetite (e.g. those of contemplation), the nature in such a case not being defective at all. That the others are incidental is indicated by the fact that men do not enjoy the same pleasant objects when their nature is in its settled state as they do when it is being replenished, but in the former case they enjoy the things that are pleasant without qualification, in the latter the contraries of these as well; for then they enjoy even sharp and bitter things, none of which is pleasant either by nature or without qualification. The states they produce, therefore, are not pleasures naturally or without qualification; for as pleasant things differ, so do the pleasures arising from them.

(X.3.3) They say, too, that pain is the lack of that which is according to nature, and pleasure is replenishment. But these experiences are bodily. If then pleasure is replenishment with that which is according to nature, that which feels pleasure will be that in which the replenishment takes place, i.e. the body; but that is not thought to be the case; therefore the replenishment is not pleasure, though one would be pleased when replenishment was taking place, just as one would be pained if one were being operated on. This opinion seems to be based on the pains and pleasures connected with nutrition; on the fact that when people have been short of food and have felt pain beforehand they are pleased by the replenishment. But this does not happen with all pleasures; for the pleasures of learning and, among the sensuous pleasures, those of smell, and also many sounds and sights, and memories and hopes, do not presuppose pain. Of what then will these be the coming into being? There has not been lack of anything of which they could be the supplying anew.

Types of Pleasures II: Unimpeded Activity That Exercises Our Faculties

(VII.12.3) Again, it is not necessary that there should be something else better than pleasure, as some say the end is better than the process; for pleasures are not processes nor do they all involve process—they are activities and ends; nor do they arise when we are becoming something, but when we are exercising some faculty; and not all pleasures have an end different from themselves, but only the pleasures of persons who are being led to the perfecting of their nature. This is why it is not right to say that pleasure is perceptible process, but it should rather be called activity of the natural state, and instead of 'perceptible,' 'unimpeded.' It is thought by some people to be process just because they think it is in the strict sense good; for they think that activity is process, which it is not.

(X.4.3) Since every sense is active in relation to its object, and a sense that is in good condition acts perfectly in relation to the most beautiful of its objects (for perfect activity seems to be ideally of this nature; whether we say that it is active, or the organ in which it resides, may be assumed to be immaterial), it follows that in the case of each sense the best activity is that of the best-conditioned organ in relation to the finest of its objects. And this activity will be the most complete and pleasant. For, while there is pleasure in respect of any sense, and in respect of thought and contemplation no less, the most complete is pleasantest, and that of a well-conditioned organ in relation to the worthiest of its objects is the most complete; and the pleasure completes the activity. But the pleasure does not complete it in the same way as the combination of object and sense, both good, just as health and the doctor are not in the same way the cause of a man's being healthy. (That pleasure is produced in respect to each sense is plain; for we speak of sights and sounds as pleasant. It is also plain that it arises most of all when both the sense is at its best and it is active in reference to an object that corresponds; when both object and perceiver are of the best there will always be pleasure, since the requisite agent and patient are both present.) Pleasure completes the activity not as the corresponding permanent state does, by its immanence, but as an end that supervenes as the bloom of youth does on those in the flower of their age. So long, then, as both the intelligible or sensible object and the discriminating or contemplative faculty are as they should be, the pleasure will be involved in the activity; for when both the passive and the active factor are unchanged and are related to each other in the same way, the same result naturally follows.

(X.4.4) How, then, is it that no one is continuously pleased? Is it that we grow weary? Certainly all human beings are incapable of continuous activity. Therefore pleasure also is not continuous; for it accompanies activity. Some things delight us when they are new, but later do so less, for the same reason; for at first the mind is in a state of stimulation and intensely active about them, as people are with respect to their vision when they look hard at a thing, but afterwards our activity is not of this kind, but has grown relaxed; for which reason the pleasure also is dulled.

(X.5.1) For this reason pleasures seem, too, to differ in kind. For things different in kind are, we think, completed by different things (we see this to be true both of natural objects and of things produced by art, e.g. animals, trees, a painting, a sculpture, a house, an implement); and, similarly, we think that activities differing in kind are completed by things differing in kind. Now the activities of thought differ from those of the senses, and both differ among themselves, in kind; so, therefore, do the pleasures that complete them.

(X.5.2) This may be seen, too, from the fact that each of the pleasures is bound up with the activity it completes. For an activity is intensified by its proper pleasure, since each class of things is better judged of and brought to precision by those who engage in the activity with pleasure; e.g. it is those who enjoy geometrical thinking that become geometers and grasp the various propositions better, and, similarly, those who are fond of music or of building, and so on, make progress in their proper function by enjoying it; so the pleasures intensify the activities, and what intensifies a thing is proper to it, but things different in kind have properties different in kind.

Bodily Pleasures

(VII.14.1) (G) With regard to the bodily pleasures, those who say that some pleasures are very much to be chosen, namely the noble pleasures, but not the bodily pleasures, i.e. those with which the self-indulgent man is concerned, must consider why, then, the contrary pains are bad. For the contrary of bad is good. Are the necessary pleasures good in the sense in which even that which is not bad is good? Or are they good up to a point? Is it that where you have states and processes of which there cannot be too much, there cannot be too much of the corresponding pleasure, and that where there can be too much of the one there can be too much of the other also? Now there can be too much of bodily goods, and the bad man is bad by virtue of pursuing the excess, not by virtue of pursuing the necessary pleasures (for all men enjoy in some way or other both dainty foods and wines and sexual intercourse, but not all men do so as they ought). The contrary is the case with pain; for he does not avoid the excess of it, he avoids it altogether; and this is peculiar to him, for the alternative to excess of pleasure is not pain, except to the man who pursues this excess.

(VII.14.2) Since we should state not only the truth but also the cause of error—for this contributes towards producing conviction, since when a reasonable explanation is given of why the false view appears true, this tends to produce belief in the true view—therefore we must state why the bodily pleasures appear the more worthy of choice. (a) Firstly, then, it is because they expel pain; owing to the excesses of pain that men experience, they pursue excessive and in general bodily pleasure as being a cure for the pain. Now curative agencies produce intense feeling—which is the reason why they are pursued—because they show up against the contrary pain. (Indeed pleasure is thought not to be good for these two reasons, as has been said, namely that (a) some of them are activities belonging to a bad nature—either congenital, as in the case of a brute, or due to habit, i.e. those of bad men; while (b) others are meant to cure a defective nature, and it is better to be in a healthy state than to be getting into it, but these arise during the process of being made perfect and are therefore only incidentally good.) (b) Further, they are pursued because of their violence by those who cannot enjoy other pleasures. (At all events they go out of their way to manufacture thirsts somehow for themselves. When these are harmless, the practice is irreproachable; when they are hurtful, it is bad.) For they have nothing else to enjoy, and, besides, a neutral state is painful to many people because of their nature. For the animal nature is always in travail, as the students of natural science also testify, saying that sight and hearing are painful; but we have become used to this, as they maintain. Similarly, while in youth people are, owing to the growth that is going on, in a situation like that of drunken men, and youth is pleasant, on the other hand people of excitable nature always need relief; for even their body is ever in torment owing to its special composition, and they are always under the influence of violent desire; but pain is driven out both by the contrary pleasure, and by any chance pleasure if it be strong; and for these reasons they become self-indulgent and bad. But the pleasures that do not involve pains do not admit of excess; and these are among the things pleasant by nature and not incidentally. By things pleasant incidentally I mean those that act as cures (for because as a result people are cured, through some action of the part that remains healthy, for this reason the process is thought pleasant); by things naturally pleasant I mean those that stimulate the action of the healthy nature.

The Good of Pleasures

(VII.13.2) And (F) if certain pleasures are bad, that does not prevent the chief good from being some pleasure, just as the chief good may be some form of knowledge though certain kinds of knowledge are bad. Perhaps it is even necessary, if each disposition has unimpeded activities, that, whether the activity (if unimpeded) of all our dispositions or that of some one of them is happiness, this should be the thing most worthy of our choice; and this activity is pleasure. Thus the chief good would be some pleasure, though most pleasures might perhaps be bad without qualification. And for this reason all men think that the happy life is pleasant and weave pleasure into their ideal of happiness—and reasonably too; for no activity is perfect when it is impeded, and happiness is a perfect thing; this is why the happy man needs the goods of the body and external goods, i.e. those of fortune, namely in order that he may not be impeded in these ways. Those who say that the victim on the rack or the man who falls into great misfortunes is happy if he is good, are, whether they mean to or not, talking nonsense. Now because we need fortune as well as other things, some people think good fortune the same thing as happiness; but it is not that, for even good fortune itself when in excess is an impediment, and perhaps should then be no longer called good fortune; for its limit is fixed by reference to happiness.

(VII.13.3) And indeed the fact that all things, both brutes and men, pursue pleasure is an indication of its being somehow the chief good:

(VII.13.5) But since no one nature or state either is or is thought the best for all, neither do all pursue the same pleasure; yet all pursue pleasure. And perhaps they actually pursue not the pleasure they think they pursue nor that which they would say they pursue, but the same pleasure; for all things have by nature something divine in them. But the bodily pleasures have appropriated the name both because we oftenest steer our course for them and because all men share in them; thus because they alone are familiar, men think there are no others.

(VII.13.6) It is evident also that if pleasure, i.e. the activity of our faculties, is not a good, it will not be the case that the happy man lives a pleasant life; for to what end should he need pleasure, if it is not a good but the happy man may even live a painful life? For pain is neither an evil nor a good, if pleasure is not; why then should he avoid it? Therefore, too, the life of the good man will not be pleasanter than that of any one else, if his activities are not more pleasant.

Good and Bad Pleasures

(X.5.3) This will be even more apparent from the fact that activities are hindered by pleasures arising from other sources. For people who are fond of playing the flute are incapable of attending to arguments if they overhear someone playing the flute, since they enjoy flute-playing more than the activity in hand; so the pleasure connected with flute-playing destroys the activity concerned with argument. This happens, similarly, in all other cases, when one is active about two things at once; the more pleasant activity drives out the other, and if it is much more pleasant does so all the more, so that one even ceases from the other. This is why when we enjoy anything very much we do not throw ourselves into anything else and do one thing only when we are not much pleased by another; e.g. in the theatre the people who eat sweets do so most when the actors are poor. Now, since activities are made precise and more enduring and better by their proper pleasure, and injured by alien pleasures, evidently the two kinds of pleasure are far apart. For alien pleasures do pretty much what proper pains do, since activities are destroyed by their proper pains; e.g. if a man finds writing or doing sums unpleasant and painful, he does not write or does not do sums, because the activity is painful. So an activity suffers contrary effects from its proper pleasures and pains, i.e. from those that supervene on it in virtue of its own nature. And alien pleasures have been stated to do much the same as pain; they destroy the activity, only not to the same degree.

(X.5.4) Now since activities differ in respect of goodness and badness, and some are worthy to be chosen, others to be avoided, and others neutral, so, too, are the pleasures; for to each activity there is a proper pleasure. The pleasure proper to a worthy activity is good and that proper to an unworthy activity bad; just as the appetites for noble objects are laudable, those for base objects culpable. But the pleasures involved in activities are more proper to them than the desires; for the latter are separated both in time and in nature, while the former are close to the activities, and so hard to distinguish from them that it admits of dispute whether the activity is not the same as the pleasure. (Still, pleasure does not seem to be thought or perception—that would be strange; but because they are not found apart they appear to some people the same.) As activities are different, then, so are the corresponding pleasures. Now sight is superior to touch in purity, and hearing and smell to taste; the pleasures, therefore, are similarly superior, and those of thought superior to these, and within each of the two kinds some are superior to others.

(X.6.2) Pleasant amusements also are thought to be of this nature; we choose them not for the sake of other things; for we are injured rather than benefited by them, since we are led to neglect our bodies and our property. But most of the people who are deemed happy take refuge in such pastimes, which is the reason why those who are ready-witted at them are highly esteemed at the courts of tyrants; they make themselves pleasant companions in the tyrants' favourite pursuits, and that is the sort of man they want. Now these things are thought to be of the nature of happiness because people in despotic positions spend their leisure in them, but perhaps such people prove nothing; for virtue and reason, from which good activities flow, do not depend on despotic position; nor, if these people, who have never tasted pure and generous pleasure, take refuge in the bodily pleasures, should these for that reason be thought more desirable; for boys, too, think the things that are valued among themselves are the best. It is to be expected, then, that, as different things seem valuable to boys and to men, so they should to bad men and to good. Now, as we have often maintained, those things are both valuable and pleasant that are such to the good man; and to each man the activity in accordance with his own disposition is most desirable, and, therefore, to the good man that which is in accordance with virtue. Happiness therefore does not lie in amusement; it would, indeed, be strange if the end were amusement, and one were to take trouble and suffer hardship all one's life in order to amuse oneself. For, in a word, everything that we choose we choose for the sake of something else—except happiness, which is an end. Now to exert oneself and work for the sake of amusement seems silly and utterly childish. But to amuse oneself in order that one may exert oneself, as Anacharsis puts it, seems right; for amusement is a sort of relaxation, and we need relaxation because we cannot work continuously. Relaxation, then, is not an end; for it is taken for the sake of activity.

(X.6.3) The happy life is thought to be virtuous; now a virtuous life requires exertion and does not consist in amusement. And we say that serious things are better than laughable things and those connected with amusement, and that the activity of the better of any two things—whether it be two elements of our being or two men—is the more serious; but the activity of the better is ipso facto superior and more of the nature of happiness. And any chance person—even a slave—can enjoy the bodily pleasures no less than the best man; but no one assigns to a slave a share in happiness—unless he assigns to him also a share in human life. For happiness does not lie in such occupations, but, as we have said before, in virtuous activities.

Confessions, Book VII

I

By now my adolescence, with all its shameful sins, was dead. I was approaching mature manhood, but the older I grew, the more disgraceful was my self-delusion. I could imagine no kind of substance except such as is normally seen by the eye. But I did not think of you, my God, in the shape of a human body, for I had rejected this idea ever since I had first begun to study philosophy, and I was glad to find that our spiritual mother, your Catholic Church, also rejected such beliefs. But I did not know how else to think of you.

I was only a man, and a weak man at that, but I tried to think of you as the supreme God, the only God, the true God. With all my heart I believed that you could never suffer decay or hurt or change, for although I did not know how or why this should be, I understood with complete certainty that what is subject to decay is inferior to that which is not, and without hesitation I placed that which cannot be harmed above that which can, and I saw that what remains constant is better than that which is changeable. My heart was full of bitter protests against the creations of my imagination, and this single truth was the only weapon with which I could try to drive from my mind's eye all the unclean images which swarmed before it. But hardly had I brushed them aside than, in the flicker of an eyelid, they crowded upon me again, forcing themselves upon my sight and clouding my vision, so that although I did not imagine you in the shape of a human body, I could not free myself from the thought that you were some kind of bodily substance extended in space, either permeating the world or diffused in infinity beyond it. This substance I thought of as something not subject to decay or harm or variation and therefore better than any that might suffer corruption or damage or change. I reasoned in this way because, if I tried to imagine something without dimensions of space, it seemed to me that nothing, absolutely nothing, remained, not even a void. For if a body were removed from the space which it occupied, and that space remained empty of any body whatsoever, whether of earth, water, air, or sky, there would still remain an empty space. Nothing would be there, but it would still be a space.

My wits were so blunt and I was so completely unable even to see clearly into my own mind, that I thought that whatever had no dimensions in space must be absolutely nothing at all. If it did not, or could not, have qualities related to space, such as density, sparseness, or bulk, I thought it must be nothing. For my mind ranged in imagination over shapes and forms such as were familiar to the eye, and I did not realize that the power of thought, by which I formed these images, was itself something quite different from them. And yet it could not form them unless it were itself something, and something great enough to do so.

So I thought of you too, O Life of my life, as a great being with dimensions extending everywhere, throughout infinite space, permeating the whole mass of the world and reaching in all directions beyond it without limit, so that the earth and the sky and all creation were full of you and their limits were within you, while you had no limits at all. For the air, that is, the atmosphere which covers the earth, is a material body, but it does not block out the light of the sun. The light passes through it and penetrates it, not by breaking it or splitting it, but by filling it completely. In the same way I imagined that you were able to pass through material bodies, not only the air and the sky and the sea, but also the earth, and that you could penetrate to all their parts, the greatest and the smallest alike, so that they were filled with your presence, and by this unseen force you ruled over all that you had created, from within and from without.

This was the theory to which I held, because I could imagine you in no other way. But it was a false theory. For if it were true, it would mean that a greater part of the earth would contain a greater part of you, and a smaller part less in proportion. Everything would be filled with your presence, but in such a way that the body of an elephant would contain more of you than the body of a sparrow, because the one is larger than the other and occupies more space. So you would distribute your parts piecemeal among the parts of the world, to each more or less according to its size. This, of course, is quite untrue. But at that time you had not yet given me light in my darkness.

2

As for the Manichees, O Lord, those frauds who deceived both themselves and others and, for all their talk, were no better than mutes because it was not your holy

Word which spoke from their lips, I could answer them well enough by using the argument which Nebridius used to put forward long ago when we were at Carthage. We had all been deeply impressed when we heard it. He used to ask what the imaginary powers of darkness, which the Manichees always describe as a force in conflict with you, would have done if you had refused to join battle with them. If they answered that this force could have done you some harm, they would, in effect, be saying that you were subject to hurt and corruption. If on the other hand they said that the powers of darkness could not harm you, there would be no purpose in a battle which was supposed to result in some part or member of you, some offshoot of your substance, becoming intermingled with opposing powers whose nature was not of your creation, and being corrupted and degraded to such an extent that its bliss was turned to misery and it needed your help if it was to be rescued and purged of evil. This offshoot of your substance, they claimed, was man's soul. It had been taken captive, made impure, and corrupted, while the Word of God, which was to come to its assistance, was free, pure and incorrupt. Yet, if this was so, the Word of God must also have been subject to corruption, because it came of one and the same substance as the soul.

Therefore, whatever you are—that is, whatever the substance by which you are what you are—if they admitted that you were incorruptible, all their theories were proved to be false and repugnant. If they said you were corruptible, it would be an obvious falsehood, no sooner uttered than rejected in horror. Nebridius' argument was therefore a sufficient answer to the Manichees, and I ought to have disgorged these men like vomit from my over-laden system, because if they thought of you and spoke of you like this, they could not extricate themselves without committing a horrible sacrilege of heart and tongue.

3

But although I declared and firmly believed that you, our Lord God, the true God who made not only our souls but also our bodies and not only our souls and bodies but all things, living and inanimate, as well, although I believed that you were free from corruption or mutation or any degree of change, I still could not find a clear explanation, without complications, of the cause of evil. Whatever the cause might be, I saw that it was not to be found in any theory that would oblige me to believe that the immutable God was mutable. If I believed this, I should myself become a cause of evil, the very thing which I was trying to discover. So I continued the search with some sense of relief, because I was quite sure that the theories of the Manichees were wrong. I repudiated these people with all my heart, because I could see that while they were inquiring into the origin of evil they were full of evil themselves, since they preferred to think that yours was a substance that could suffer evil rather than that theirs was capable of committing it.

I was told that we do evil because we choose to do so of our own free will, and suffer it because your justice rightly demands that we should. I did my best to understand this, but I could not see it clearly. I tried to raise my mental perceptions out of the abyss which engulfed them, but I sank back into it once more. Again and again I tried, but always I sank back. One thing lifted me up into the light of your day. It was that I knew that I had a will, as surely as I knew that there was life in me. When I chose to do something or not to do it, I was quite certain that it was my own self, and not some other person, who made this act of will, so that I was on the point of understanding that herein lay the cause of my sin. If I did anything against my will, it seemed to me to be something which happened to me rather than something which I did, and I looked upon it not as a fault, but as a punishment. And because I thought of you as a just God, I admitted at once that your punishments were not unjust.

But then I would ask myself once more: 'Who made me? Surely it was my God, who is not only good but Goodness itself. How, then, do I come to possess a will that can choose to do wrong and refuse to do good, thereby providing a just reason why I should be punished? Who put this will into me? Who sowed this seed of bitterness in me, when all that I am was made by my God, who is Sweetness itself? If it was the devil who put it there, who made the devil? If he was a good angel who became a devil because of his own wicked will, how did he come to possess the wicked will which made him a devil, when the Creator, who is entirely good, made him a good angel and nothing else?'

These thoughts swept me back again into the gulf where I was being stifled. But I did not sink as far as that hell of error where no one confesses to you his own guilt, choosing to believe that you suffer evil rather than that man does it.

4

Now that I had realized that what is incorruptible is better than that which is not, I took this as the basis for further research and acknowledged that, whatever your nature might be, you must be incorruptible. For no soul has ever been, or ever will be, able to conceive of anything better than you, who are the supreme, the perfect Good. And since, as I now believed, there could be no possible doubt that the incorruptible is better than the corruptible, it followed that you must be incorruptible; otherwise I should be able to think of something that was better than my God. So, once I had seen that the incorruptible is superior to the corruptible, I had to search for you in the light of this truth and make it the starting point of my inquiry into the origin of evil, that is, the origin of corruption, by which your substance cannot possibly be violated. For there is no means whatsoever by which corruption can injure our God, whether by an act of will, by necessity, or by chance. This is because he is God and what he wills is good and he is himself that same

Good: whereas to be corrupted is not good. And you are never compelled, my God, to do or suffer anything against your will, because your will is not greater than your power. It would be greater only if you were greater than yourself, for the will and power of God are God himself. Neither can anything unforeseen happen to you, because you know all things and nothing, whatever its nature, exists except by reason of the very fact that you know it. Need I say more to prove that the substance which is God cannot be corruptible since, if it were, it would not be God?

5

I was trying to find the origin of evil, but I was quite blind to the evil in my own method of research. In my mind's eye I pictured the whole of creation, but the things which are visible to us, such as the earth and the sea, the air and the stars, the trees and the animals which live their lives and die, and the things which we cannot see, such as the firmament of Heaven above, with all its angels and everything in it that is spiritual—for I thought of spiritual things, too, as material bodies, each in its allotted place. I imagined the whole of your creation as a vast mass made up of different kinds of bodies, some of them real, some of them only the bodies which in my imagination took the place of spirits. I thought of this mass as something huge. I could not, of course, know how big it really was, but I made it as large as need be, though finite in all directions. I pictured you, O Lord, as encompassing this mass on all sides and penetrating it in every part, yet yourself infinite in every dimension. It was as though there were sea everywhere, nothing but an immense, an infinite sea, and somewhere within it a sponge, as large as might be but not infinite, filled through and through with the water of this boundless sea. In some such way as this I imagined that your creation, which was finite, was filled by you, who were infinite. I said to myself, 'Here is God, and here is what he has created. God is good, utterly and entirely better than the things which he has made. But, since he is good, the things that he has made are also good. This is how he contains them all in himself and fills them all with his presence.

'Where then is evil? What is its origin? How did it steal into the world? What is the root or seed from which it grew? Can it be that there simply is no evil? If so, why do we fear and guard against something which is not there? If our fear is unfounded, it is itself an evil, because it stabs and wrings our hearts for nothing. In fact the evil is all the greater if we are afraid when there is nothing to fear. Therefore, either there is evil and we fear it, or the fear itself is evil.

'Where then does evil come from, if God made all things and, because he is good, made them good too? It is true that he is the supreme Good, that he is himself a greater Good than these lesser goods which he created. But the Creator and all his creation are both good. Where then does evil come from?

'Can it be that there was something evil in the matter from which he made the universe? When he shaped this matter and fitted it to his purpose, did he leave in it some part which he did not convert to good? But why should he have done this? Are we to believe that, although he is omnipotent, he had not the power to convert the whole of this matter to good and change it so that no evil remained in it? Why, indeed, did he will to make anything of it at all? Why did he not instead, by this same omnipotence, destroy it utterly and entirely? Could it have existed against his will? If it had existed from eternity, why did he allow it to exist in that state through the infinite ages of the past and then, after so long a time, decide to make something of it? If he suddenly determined to act, would it not be more likely that he would use his almighty power to abolish this evil matter, so that nothing should exist besides himself, the total, true, supreme, and infinite Good? Or, if it was not good that a God who was good should not also create and establish something good, could he not have removed and annihilated the evil matter and replaced it with good, of which he could create all things? For he would not be omnipotent if he could not create something good without the help of matter which he had not created himself.'

These were the thoughts which I turned over and over in my unhappy mind, and my anxiety was all the more galling for the fear that death might come before I had found the truth. But my heart clung firmly to the faith in Christ your Son, our Lord and Saviour, which it had received in the Catholic Church. There were many questions on which my beliefs were still indefinite and wavered from the strict rule of doctrine, yet my mind never relinquished the faith but drank it in more deeply day by day.

6

By this time I had also turned my back upon the astrologers with their illusory claims to predict the future and their insane and impious ritual. In this too, my God, let me acknowledge your mercy from the deepest depths of my soul! For you, and you alone, are the life that recalls us from the death we die each time we err. You alone are the life which never dies and the wisdom that needs no light besides itself, but illumines all who need to be enlightened, the wisdom that governs the world, down to the leaves that flutter on the trees.

You provided me with a friend who cured my stubborn resistance both to that wise old man Vindicianus[1] and to Nebridius who, for all his youth, was gifted with spiritual qualities that I greatly admired. Vindicianus was quite outspoken on the subject of astrology. Nebridius was not so ready to declare himself, although he too repeated often enough that there was no art by which the future could be foretold. They said that guesswork was often borne out by mere chance. If a man made a great many predictions, several of them would later prove to be true, but he could not know it at the time and would only hit upon them by chance, simply by opening his mouth to speak.

So to cure my obstinacy you found me a friend who was usually ready enough to consult the astrologers. He had made no real study of their lore but, as I have said, he used to make inquiries of them out of curiosity. He did this although he was perfectly well aware of certain facts about them which he said he had heard from his father. If only he had realized it, these facts would have been quite enough to destroy his belief in astrology.

This man, whose name was Firminus, had been educated in the liberal arts and had received a thorough training in rhetoric. He came to consult me, as his closest friend, about some business matters of which he had high hopes, and asked me what prospects I could see in his horoscope, as they call it. I was already beginning to change my mind in favor of Nebridius's opinions on astrology, but I did not refuse outright to read the stars for him and tell him what I saw, though I had little faith in it myself. Nevertheless I added that I was almost convinced that it was all absurd and quite meaningless. He then told me that his father had studied books of astrology with the greatest interest and had had a friend who shared his enthusiasm for the subject. Each was as intent upon this nonsense as the other, and by pooling their experiences they whetted their enthusiasm to the point that, even when their domestic animals had litters, they would note the exact moment of birth and record the position of the stars, intending to use these observations for their experiments in this so-called art.

Firminus went on to tell me a story about his own birth. His father had told him that when his mother was pregnant, a female slave in the household of this friend was also expecting a child. Her master was of course aware of her condition, because he used to take very great care to find out even when his dogs were due to have puppies. The two men made the most minute calculations to determine the time of labor of both the women, counting the days, the hours, and even the minutes, and it so happened that both gave birth at exactly the same moment. This meant that the horoscopes which they cast for the two babies had to be exactly the same, down to the smallest particular, though one was the son of the master of the house and the other a slave. For as soon as labor began, each man informed the other of the situation in his house, and each had a messenger waiting, ready to be sent to the other as soon as the birth was announced. As the confinements took place in their own houses, they could easily arrange to be told without delay. The messengers, so Firminus told me, crossed paths at a point which was exactly half way between the two houses, so that each of the two friends inevitably made an identical observation of the stars and could not find the least difference in the time of birth. Yet Firminus, who was born of a rich family, strode along the smoother paths of life. His wealth increased and high honours came his way. But the slave continued to serve his masters. Firminus, who knew him, said that his lot had been in no way bettered.

I believed this story when I heard it, because Firminus was a man whom I could trust. It marked the final end of all my doubts, and my first reaction was to try to redeem Firminus from his interest in astrology. I told him that if I had cast his horoscope and my reading of the stars was correct, I could only have seen in them that his parents were important people, that he belonged to one of the noble families of his town, that he was a freeman by birth, that his upbringing suited his rank, and that his education was liberal. But the slave was born under the very same constellations, and if he had asked me to tell him their meaning, my interpretation of them could not have been true unless I saw in them a family of the meanest sort, the status of a slave, and various other details entirely different from and inconsistent with those which applied to Firminus. This proved that if I were to say what was actually the truth, I should give a different answer to each, though the stars I read were the same; whereas, if I gave the same answer to each, I should be wrong in fact. It was therefore perfectly clear to me that when predictions based on observations of the stars turn out to be true, it is a matter of luck, not of skill. When they turn out to be wrong, it is not due to lack of skill, but to the perversity of chance.

Taking this as my starting point I began to think the matter over in my mind, so that I should have an answer ready if the eccentrics who made their living at this trade should raise the objection that the story, as Firminus told it, was untrue, or that he had been misinformed by his father. By now I was eager to move to the attack and reduce these people to silence by ridicule. So I turned my attention to the case of twins, who are generally born within a short time of each other. Whatever significance in the natural order the astrologers may attribute to this interval of time, it is too short to be appreciated by human observation and no allowance can be made for it in the charts which an astrologer has to consult in order to cast a true horoscope. His predictions, then, will not be true, because he would have consulted the same charts for both Esau and Jacob and would have made the same predictions for each of them, whereas it is a fact that the same things did not happen to them both. Therefore, either he would have been wrong in his predictions or, if his forecast was correct, he would not have predicted the same future for each. And yet he would have consulted the same chart in each case. This proves that if he had foretold the truth, it would have been by luck, not by skill. For, O Lord, though neither the astrologers nor those who consult them know it, by your secret prompting each man, when he seeks their advice, hears what it is right for him to hear. For you rule the universe with the utmost justice, and in the inscrutable depths of your just judgement you know what is right for him, because you can see the hidden merits of our souls. And let no man question the why or the wherefore of your judgment. This he must not do, for his is only a man.

7

By now, O God my Help, you had released me by this means from the bondage of astrology. But I was still trying to discover the origin of evil, and I could find no solution to the problem. My ideas were always changing, like the ebb and flow of the tide, but you never allowed them to sweep me away from the faith by which I believed that you were, that your substance was unchangeable, and that it was yours to care for and to judge mankind. I believed too that it was in Christ your Son, our Lord, and in the Holy Scriptures, which are affirmed by the authority of your Catholic Church, that you had laid the path of man's salvation, so that he might come to that other life which is to follow this our life in death. These beliefs remained intact and firmly rooted in my mind, but I was still burning with anxiety to find the source from which evil comes.

What agony I suffered, my God! How I cried out in grief, while my heart was in labor! But, unknown to me, you were there, listening. Even when I bore the pain of my search valiantly, in silence, the mute sufferings of my soul were loud voices calling to your mercy. You knew what I endured, but no man knew. How little of it could I find words to tell, even to my closest friends! Could they catch a sound of the turmoil in my soul? Time did not suffice to tell them and words failed me. But as *I groaned aloud in the wariness of my heart*,[2] all my anguish reached your ears. *You knew all my longings; the very light that shone in my eyes was mine no longer.*[2] For the light was within, while I looked on the world outside. The light was not in space, but I thought only of things that are contained in space, and in them I found no place where I might rest. They offered me no haven where I could own myself satisfied and content, nor would they let me turn back where I might find contentment and satisfaction. For I was a creature of a higher order than these things, though I was lower than you. You were my true Joy while I was subject to you, and you had made subject to me all the things that you had created inferior to me. This was the right mean, the middle path that led to my salvation, if only I remained true to your likeness and, by serving you, became the master of my own body. But when I rose in pride against you and *made onslaught* against my Lord, *proud of my strong sinews*,[3] even those lower things became my masters and oppressed me, and nowhere could I find respite or time to draw my breath. Everywhere I looked they loomed before my eyes in swarms and clusters, and when I set myself to thinking and tried to escape from them, images of these self-same things blocked my way, as though they were asking where I meant to go, unclean and undeserving as I was. All this had grown from my wound, for the proud *lie wounded at your feet*,[4] and I was separated from you by the swelling of my pride, as though my cheeks were so puffed with conceit that they masked the sight of my eyes.

8

O Lord, you are eternal but you will not *always be indignant with us,*[5] because you take pity on our dust and ashes. You saw me and it pleased you to transform all that was misshapen in me. Your goad was thrusting at my heart, giving me no peace until the eye of my soul could discern you without mistake. Under the secret touch of your healing hand my swelling pride subsided, and day by day the pain I suffered brought me health, like an ointment which stung but cleared the confusion and darkness from the eye of my mind.

9

First of all it was your will to make me understand how *you thwart the proud and keep your grace for the humble*[6] and what a great act of your mercy it was to show mankind the way of humility when *the Word was made flesh and came to dwell*[7] among the men of this world. So you made use of a man, one who was bloated with the most outrageous pride, to procure me some of the books of the Platonists, translated from the Greek into Latin. In them I read—not, of course, word for word, though the sense was the same and it was supported by all kinds of different arguments—that *at the beginning of time the Word already was; and God had the Word abiding with him, and the Word was God. He abode, at the beginning of time, with God. It was through him that all things came into being, and without him came nothing that has come to be. In him there was life, and that life was the light of men. And the light shines in darkness, a darkness which was not able to master it.* I read too that the soul of man, although it *bears witness of the light, is not the Light* But the Word, who is himself God, is *the true Light, which enlightens every soul born into the world. He, through whom the world was made, was in the world, and the world treated him as a stranger.* But I did not find it written in those books that *he came to what was his own, and they who were his own gave him no welcome. But all those who did welcome him he empowered to become the children of God, all those who believe in his name.*[8]

In the same books I also read of the Word, God, that his *birth came not from human stock, not from nature's will or man's, but from God.*[8] But I did not read in them that the Word was made flesh and came to dwell among us.[8]

Though the words were different and the meaning was expressed in various ways, I also learned from these books that God the Son, being himself, like the Father, of divine nature, *did not see, in the rank of Godhead, a prize to be coveted.*[9] But they do not say that *he dispossessed himself, and took the nature of a slave, fashioned in the likeness of men, and presenting himself to us in human form;*

and then he lowered his own dignity, accepted an obedience which brought him to death, death on a cross; and that is why God has raised him from the dead, given him that name which is greater than any other name; so that everything in heaven and on earth and under the earth must bend the knee before the name of Jesus, and every tongue must confess Jesus Christ as the Lord, dwelling in the glory of God the Father.[10]

The books also tell us that your only-begotten Son abides for ever in eternity with you; that before all time began, he was; that he is above all time and suffers no change; that of his plenty our souls receive their part[11] and hence derive their blessings; and that by partaking of the Wisdom which abides in them they are renewed, and this is the source of their wisdom. But there is no word in those books to say that *in his own appointed time he underwent death for us sinners*[12] and that *you did not even spare your own Son, but gave him up for us all.*[13] For *you have hidden all this from the wise and revealed it to little children,* so that *all that labor and are burdened may come to him and he will give them rest,* because *he is gentle and humble of heart;*[14] and *in his own laws he will train the humble, in his own paths the humble he will guide,*[15] for he sees how we are *restless and forlorn* and is *merciful to our sins.*[16] But some hold their heads so high in the clouds of learning that they do not hear him saying *Learn from me; I am gentle and humble of heart; and you shall find rest for your souls.*[17] *Although they have the knowledge of God, they do not honour him or give thanks to him as God, they become fantastic in their notions, and their senseless hearts grow benighted; they, who claim to be so wise, turn fools.*[18]

I read too in the same books that *they had exchanged the glory of the imperishable Gods*[18] for idols and all kinds of make-believe, *for representations of perishable man, of bird and beast and reptile,*[18] in fact for that Egyptian food for which Esau lost his birthright, since your first-born people worshipped the head of a four-footed beast instead of you and, *turning their thoughts towards Egypt,*[19] bowed down their souls, those images made in your likeness, before the *semblance of a bullock at grass.*[20] All this I found in those books, but I did not feed upon this fare. For it pleased you, Lord, to rid Jacob of the reproach of inferiority so that *the elder should be the servant of the younger,*[21] and you have called the Gentiles into your inheritance. It was from the Gentiles that I had come to you, and I set my mind upon the gold which you willed your people to carry away from Egypt for, wherever it was, it was yours. Through your apostle you told the Athenians that *it is in you that we live and move and have our being, as some of their own poets have told us.*[22] And, of course, the books I was reading were written in Athens. But your people had used the gold that was yours to serve the idols of the Egyptians, for *they had exchanged God's truth for a lie, reverencing and worshipping the creature in preference to the Creator,*[18] and it was not upon these idols that I set my mind.

10

These books served to remind me to return to my own self. Under your guidance I entered into the depths of my soul, and this I was able to do because *your aid befriended me.*[23] I entered, and with the eye of my soul, such as it was, I saw the Light that never changes casting its rays over the same eye of my soul, over my mind. It was not the common light of day that is seen by the eye of every living thing of flesh and blood, nor was it some more spacious light of the same sort, as if the light of day were to shine far, far brighter than it does and fill all space with a vast brilliance. What I saw was something quite, quite different from any light we know on earth. It shone above my mind, but not in the way that oil floats above water or the sky hangs over the earth. It was above me because it was itself the Light that made me, and I was below because I was made by it. All who know the truth know this Light, and all who know this Light know eternity. It is the Light that charity knows.

Eternal Truth, true Love, beloved Eternity—all this, my God, you are, and it is to you that I sigh by night and day. When first I knew you, you raised me up so that I could see that there was something to be seen, but also that I was not yet able to see it. I gazed on you with eyes too weak to resist the dazzle of your splendour. Your light shone upon me in its brilliance, and I thrilled with love and dread alike. I realized that I was far away from you. It was as though I were in a land where all is different from your own, and I heard your voice calling from on high, saying 'I am the food of full-grown men. Grow and you shall feed on me. But you shall not change me into your own substance, as you do with the food of your body. Instead you shall be changed into me.' I realized too that you have chastened man for his sins[24]; you made my life melt away like gossamer,[24] and I asked myself 'Is truth then nothing at all, simply because it has no extension in space, with or without limits?' And, far off, I heard your voice saying *I am the God who IS.*[25] I heard your voice, as we hear voices that speak to our hearts, and at once I had no cause to doubt. I might more easily have doubted that I was alive than that Truth had being. For we catch sight of the Truth, as he is known through his creation.[26]

11

Also I considered all the other things that are of a lower order than yourself, and I saw that they have not absolute being in themselves, nor are they entirely without being. They are real in so far as they have their being from you, but unreal in the sense that they are not what you are. For it is only that which remains in being without change that truly is. As for me, *I know no other content but clinging to God,*[27] because unless my being remains in him, it cannot remain in me. But *himself ever unchanged, he makes all things new.*[28] *I own him as my God; he has no need of ought that is mine.*[29]

12

It was made clear to me also that even those things which are subject to decay are good. If they were of the supreme order of goodness, they could not become corrupt; but neither could they become corrupt unless they were in some way good. For if they were supremely good, it would not be possible for them to be corrupted. On the other hand, if they were entirely without good, there would be nothing in them that could become corrupt. For corruption is harmful, but unless it diminished what is good, it could do no harm. The conclusion then must be either that corruption does no harm—which is not possible; or that everything which is corrupted is deprived of good—which is beyond doubt. But if they are deprived of all good, they will not exist at all. For if they still exist but can no longer be corrupted, they will be better than they were before, because they now continue their existence in an incorruptible state. But could anything be more preposterous than to say that things are made better by being deprived of all good?

So we must conclude that if things are deprived of all good, they cease altogether to be; and this means that as long as they are, they are good. Therefore, whatever is, is good; and evil, the origin of which I was trying to find, is not a substance, because if it were a substance, it would be good. For either it would be an incorruptible substance of the supreme order of goodness, or it would be a corruptible substance which would not be corruptible unless it were good. So it became obvious to me that all that you have made is good, and that there are no substances whatsoever that were not made by you. And because you did not make them all equal, each single thing is good and collectively they are very good, for our God made his whole creation *very good.*[30]

13

For you evil does not exist, and not only for you but for the whole of your creation as well, because there is nothing outside it which could invade it and break down the order which you have imposed on it. Yet in the separate parts of your creation there are some things which we think of as evil because they are at variance with other things. But there are other things again with which they are in accord, and then they are good. In themselves, too, they are good. And all these things which are at variance with one another are in accord with the lower part of creation which we call the earth. The sky, which is cloudy and windy, suits the earth to which it belongs. So it would be wrong for me to wish that these earthly things did not exist, for even if I saw nothing but them, I might wish for something better, but still I ought to praise you for them alone. For all things *give praise to the Lord on earth, monsters of the sea and all its depths; fire and hail, snow and mist, and the storm-wind that executes his decree; all you mountains and hills, all you fruit trees and cedars; all you wild beasts and cattle, creeping things and birds that fly in air, all you kings and peoples of the world, all you that are princes and judges on earth; young men and maids, old men and boys together; let them all give praise to the Lord's name.*[31] The heavens, too, ring with your praises, O God, for you are the God of us all. *Give praise to the Lord in heaven; praise him, all that dwells on high. Praise him, all you angels of his, praise him, all his armies. Praise him, sun and moon; praise him, every star that shines. Praise him, you highest heavens, you waters beyond the heavens. Let all these praise the Lord.*[32] And since this is so, I no longer wished for a better world, because I was thinking of the whole of creation, and in the light of this clearer discernment I had come to see that though the higher things are better than the lower, the sum of all creation is better than the higher things alone.

14

Those who find fault with any part of your creation are bereft of reason, just as I was when I decried many of the things which you had made. My soul did not dare to find fault with my God, and therefore it would not admit that what it found distasteful had been created by you. This was why it went astray and accepted the theory of the two substances. This, too, was why it could find no rest and talked so foolishly. Then it had turned away from this error and had imagined for itself a god extended through all space to infinity. Thinking that this god was you, it had enshrined this idol in its heart and, once again, had made of itself a temple abominable to you. But, unknown to me, you soothed my head and closed my eyes so that they should not look upon *vain phantoms,*[33] and I became drowsy and slept away my madness. I awoke in you and saw that you were infinite, but not in the way I had supposed. This I saw, but it was not with the sight of the flesh that I saw it.

15

I looked at other things too and saw that they owe their being to you. I saw that all finite things are in you, not as though you were a place that contained them, but in a different manner. They are in you because you hold all things in your truth as though they were in your hand, and all things are true in so far as they have being. Falsehood is nothing but the supposed existence of something which has no being.

I saw too that all things are fit and proper not only to the places but also to the times in which they exist, and that you, who are the only eternal Being, did not begin to work only after countless ages of time had elapsed, because no age of time, past or still to come, could either come or go if it were not that you abide for ever and cause time to come and go.

16

From my own experience I knew that there was nothing strange in the fact that a man who finds bread agreeable to the taste when he is well finds it hard to eat when he is sick, and that light is hateful to sore eyes, although we welcome it when our sight is hale and clear. In the same way the wicked find your justice disagreeable, just as they find vipers and worms unpleasant. Yet these animals were created good by you. They were created to suit the lower order of your creation. Thus the wicked themselves are suited to this lower order in as much as they are unlike you, whereas they are suited to the higher order in so far as they become more like you. And when I asked myself what wickedness was, I saw that it was not a substance but perversion of the will when it turns aside from you, O God, who are the supreme substance, and veers towards things of the lowest order, being *bowelled alive*[34] and becoming inflated with desire for things outside itself.

17

I was astonished that although I now loved you and not some phantom in your place, I did not persist in enjoyment of my God. Your beauty drew me to you, but soon I was dragged away from you by my own weight and in dismay I plunged again into the things of this world. The weight I carried was the habit of the flesh. But your memory remained with me and I had no doubt at all that you were the one to whom I should cling, only I was not yet able to cling to you. For *ever the soul is weighed down by a mortal body, earthbound cell that clogs the manifold activity of its thought.*[35] I was most certain, too, that *from the foundations of the world men have caught sight of your invisible nature, your eternal power, and your divineness, as they are known through your creatures.*[35] For I wondered how it was that I could appreciate beauty in material things on earth or in the heavens, and what it was that enabled me to make correct decisions about things that are subject to change and to rule that one thing ought to be like this, another like that. I wondered how it was that I was able to judge them in this way, and I realized that above my own mind, which was liable to change, there was the never changing, true eternity of truth. So, step by step, my thoughts moved on from the consideration of material things to the soul, which perceives things through the senses of the body, and then to the soul's inner power, to which the bodily senses communicate external facts. Beyond this dumb animals cannot go. The next stage is the power of reason, to which the facts communicated by the bodily senses are submitted for judgment.

This power of reason, realizing that in me it too was liable to change, led me on to consider the source of its own understanding. It withdrew my thoughts from their normal course and drew back from the confusion of images which pressed upon it, so that it might discover what light it was that had been shed upon it when it proclaimed for certain that what was immutable was better than that which was not, and how it had come to know the immutable itself. For unless, by some means, it had known the immutable, it could not possibly have been certain that it was preferable to the mutable. And so, in an instant of awe, my mind attained to the sight of the God who IS. Then, at last, *I caught sight of your invisible nature, as it is known through your creatures.*[36] But I had no strength to fix my gaze upon them. In my weakness I recoiled and fell back into my old ways, carrying with me nothing but the memory of something that I loved and longed for, as though I had sensed the fragrance of the fare but was not yet able to eat it.

18

I began to search for a means of gaining the strength I needed to enjoy you, but I could not find this means until I embraced the *mediator between God and men, Jesus Christ, who is a man, like them,*[37] and also *rules as God over all things, blessed for ever.*[38] He was calling to me and saying *I am the way; I am truth and life.*[39] He it was who united with our flesh that food which I was too weak to take; for *the Word was made flesh*[40] so that your Wisdom, by which you created all things, might be milk to suckle us in infancy. For I was not humble enough to conceive of the humble Jesus Christ as my God, nor had I learnt what lesson his human weakness was meant to teach. The lesson is that your Word, the eternal Truth, which far surpasses even the higher parts of your creation, raises up to himself all who subject themselves to him. From the clay of which we are made he built for himself a lowly house in this world below, so that by this means he might cause those who were to be made subject to him to abandon themselves and come over to his side. He would cure them of the pride that swelled upon their hearts and would nurture love in its place, so that they should no longer stride ahead confident in themselves but might realize their own weakness when at their feet they saw God himself, enfeebled by sharing this garment of our mortality. And at last, from weariness, they would cast themselves down upon his humanity, and when it rose they too would rise.

19

But my mind was filled with thoughts of another kind. I thought of Christ, my Lord, as no more than a man of extraordinary wisdom, whom none could equal. In particular, I saw his miraculous birth of a virgin mother, by which he showed us that worldly goods are to be despised for the sake of immortal life, as an act of the divine providence which looks after us, so that by it he merited his special authority as our Teacher. But I had not even an inkling of the meaning of the mystery of the Word made flesh. From what the Scriptures record of him, that is, that he ate and drank, that he slept and walked, that he was sometimes happy, sometimes sad, and that he preached his gospel, all I had learnt was that when your Word took human flesh, he must also have taken a human soul and a human mind. This much is known to all who know that your Word cannot suffer change, as by now I knew in so far as I was able to know it. In fact I had no doubt of it at all. For to move the limbs of the body at one moment, and at the next to hold them still; to feel some emotion and then not to feel it; at one instant to utter words which convey an intelligible meaning, and at another to remain silent—all these characteristics show that there is the possibility of change in the mind and in the soul. If they were falsely attributed to Christ in the records of his life, the whole of Scripture would be open to the charge of falsehood and mankind could no longer place any sure faith in it. So, granted that what the Scriptures say is true, I accepted that Christ was perfect man. I did not think of him as having only the body of man or man's body and sensitive soul without his reasoning mind, but as a man complete. And I thought he was superior to other men, not because he was Truth in person, but because in him human nature had reached the highest point of excellence and he had a more perfect share of divine wisdom.

Alypius, on the other hand, thought that Catholics believed that God was clothed in the flesh in the sense that in Christ there was the Godhead and the flesh but no soul. He did not think that their teaching was that Christ had a human mind, and his approach to the Christian faith itself was delayed because he found it a convincing argument that the actions recorded of Christ could only have been performed by a creature endowed with vitality and the power of reason. Later on he realized that this was the error of the Apollinarian heretics and he then gladly accepted the Catholic faith. As for me, I must confess that it was not until later that I learned how true Catholic doctrine differs from the error of Photinus in interpreting the meaning of the incarnation. It is indeed true that the refutation of heretics gives greater prominence to the tenets of your Church and the principles of sound doctrine. *For parties there must needs be, so that those who are true metal may be distinguished from the rest.*[41]

20

By reading these books of the Platonists I had been prompted to look for truth as something incorporeal, and I *caught sight of your invisible nature, as it is known through your creatures.*[42] Though I was thwarted of my wish to know more, I was conscious of what it was that my mind was too clouded to see. I was certain both that you are and that you are infinite, though without extent in terms of space either limited or unlimited. I was sure that it is you who truly are, since you are always the same, varying in neither part nor motion. I knew too that all other things derive their being from you, and the one indisputable proof of this is the fact that they exist at all. I was quite certain of these truths, but I was too weak to enjoy you. I used to talk glibly as though I knew the meaning of it all, but unless I had looked for the way which leads to you in Christ our Saviour, instead of finding knowledge I should have found my end. For I had now begun to wish to be thought wise. I was full of self-esteem, which was a punishment of my own making. I ought to have deplored my state, but instead my *knowledge only bred self-conceit.*[43] For was I not without charity, which builds its edifice on the firm foundation of humility, that is, on Jesus Christ?[44] But how could I expect that the Platonist books would ever teach me charity? I believe that it was by your will that I came across those books before I studied the Scriptures, because you wished me always to remember the impression they had made on me, so that later on, when I had been chastened by your Holy Writ and my wounds had been touched by your healing hand, I should be able to see and understand the difference between presumption and confession, between those. who see the goal that they must reach, but cannot see the road by which they are to reach it, and those who see the road to that blessed country which is meant to be no mere vision but our home. For if I had not come across these books until after I had been formed in the mould of your Holy Scriptures and had learnt to love you through familiarity with them, the Platonist teaching might have swept me from my foothold on the solid ground of piety, and even if I had held firm to the spirit in which the Scriptures had imbued me for my salvation, I might have thought it possible for a man who read nothing but the Platonist books to derive the same spirit from them alone.

21

So I seized eagerly upon the venerable writings inspired by your Holy Spirit, especially those of the apostle Paul. At one time it had seemed to me that he sometimes contradicted himself and that the purport of his words did not agree with the evidence of the law and the prophets, but these difficulties now disappeared once and for all. I saw clearly that his sober discourse pointed to one meaning only, and I learned to *rejoice with awe in my heart.*[45] I began to read and discovered that whatever truth I had found in the Platonists was set down here as well, and with it here was praise for your grace bestowed. For Saint Paul teaches that he who sees ought not to boast as though what he sees, and even the power by which he sees, *had not come to him by gift.*[46] For, whatever powers he has, *did they not come to him by gift?*[46] By the gift of grace he is now only shown how to see you, who are always the same, but is also given the strength to hold you. By your grace, too, if he is far from you and cannot see you, he is enabled to walk upon the path that leads him closer to you, so that he may see you and hold you. For even if a man *inwardly applauds God's disposition,*[47] how is he to resist *that other disposition is his lower self, which raises war against the disposition of his conscience, so that he is handed over as a captive to that disposition towards sin, which his lower self contains?*[48] For *you have right on your side, O Lord, but we are sinners, that have wronged and forsaken you; all is amiss with us.*[49] *We are bowed down by your chastisement.*[50] In justice we have been delivered to the author of sin, the prince of death, because he has coaxed us to make our wills conform with his, for *he has never taken his stand upon your truth.*[51] What is man to do in this plight? *Who is to set him free from a nature thus doomed to death? Nothing else than the grace of God, through Jesus Christ our Lord,*[52] who was begotten by you to be co-eternal with yourself and whom you made *when first you went about your work.*[53] In him the prince of this world found no crime worthy of death:[54] yet he slew him, and thus *the decree made to our prejudice was cancelled.*[55]

None of this is contained in the Platonists' books. Their pages have not the mien of the true love of God. They make no mention of the tears of confession or of *the sacrifice that you will never disdain, a broken spirit, a heart that is humbled and contrite*[56] nor do they speak of the salvation of your people, *the city adorned like a bride,*[57] *the foretaste of your Spirit,*[58] or the chalice of our redemption. In them no one sings *No rest has my soul but in God's hands; to him I look for deliverance. I have no other stronghold, no other deliverer but him; safe in his protection, I fear no deadly fall.*[59] In them no one listens to the voice which says *Come to me all you that labour.*[60] They disdain his teaching because *he is gentle and humble of heart. For you have hidden all this from the wise and revealed it to little children.*[60]

It is one thing to descry the land of peace from a wooded hilltop and, unable to find the way to it, struggle on through trackless wastes where traitors and runaways, captained by their prince, who is *lion and serpent*[61] in one, lie in wait to attack. It is another thing to follow the high road to that land of peace, the way that is defended by the care of the heavenly Commander. Here there are no deserters from heaven's army to prey upon the traveller, because they shun this road as a torment.

It was wonderful how these truths came home to me when I read *the least of your apostles*[62] and the thought of your works had set my heart trembling.

The Ancient World to 44 B.C.E.

Year	Rome and Italian Peninsula	Greece	The Near East
9000–2000 B.C.E.		First farms in Greece ca. 6500; Cycladic culture 3200–2000	9000–8000: "Neolithic Revolution" (animals and crops domesticated)
2000–1500 B.C.E.		Minoan culture thrives	Kingdom of Hammurabi
1500–1300 B.C.E.	Mycenaean settlements		
1300–1100 B.C.E.		"Trojan War"	
1100–700 B.C.E.	Phoenician settlements	Phoenician syllabary leads to Greek alphabet; Oracle of Apollo becomes central; hoplite warfare develops; Olympic Games (776)	Kingdom of David and Solomon, 10th century; Phoenicians active, develop syllabary
700–600 B.C.E.	Etruscans active, gradually succumb to Rome (founded 753)	Colonization in Mediterranean and Black Sea; Greek tyrants; Sappho active	Babylonians conquer Nineveh
600–500 B.C.E.	Roman Republic founded 510	Cleisthenes develops first known democratic government	Rise of Persia, fall of Babylon 539; Persian Empire
500–400 B.C.E.		Persian Wars; Peloponnesian War; Athens' "Golden Age" (Pericles, Sophocles, Thucydides, Socrates)	

The Ancient World to 44 B.C.E. (continued)

Year	Rome and Italian Peninsula	Greece	The Near East
400–300 B.C.E.	Celts active; conflict with Romans; Roman wars with neighbors		
300–200 B.C.E.	Rome conquers Italian peninsula; Wars with Carthage	Successors of Alexander rule in Greece, Egypt, Asia Minor; Greek language spreads	
200–100 B.C.E.	By 100, Roman Empire extends to Spain, southern Gaul, Greece and Asia Minor		
100–44 B.C.E.	Conquest of Gaul; death of Julius Caesar 44		

Ancient World, 44 B.C.E.–750 C.E.

	Rome	Greece	Egypt and Near East
44 B.C.E.–100 C.E.	Roman Republic replaced by Principate; conquest of Britain; Vesuvius destroys Pompeii 79 C.E.		Palestine becomes Roman province, 6 CE; Jesus born in Bethlehem; Herod "The Great" rules 37–4 B.C.E.; St. Paul active 46–60 C.E.; Romans destroy Temple in Jerusalem, 70
100–400 C.E.	Roman empire reaches Persian Gulf; Germans invade Roman possessions; Christianity becomes official religion of Rome 313.		Mishnah develops, Jewish Revolt 132 and subsequent diaspora; various persecutions of Christians
400–600 C.E.	Goths and Vandals invade in western Europe; Alaric sacks Rome	Roman Empire based in Constantinople; Justinian reconquers northern Italy; rise of Papacy	
600–750 C.E.			Islamic calendar begins 622; Mohammed dies 632; massive Arab expansion through N. Africa and Spain

The Renaissance

1300–1450	Black Death 1346–53 ravages Europe Cosimo de'Medici uses fortune of one of Europe's wealthiest families to patronize the arts and found the Platonic Academy in Florence Dante, Petrarch, Giotto active in Italy, Chaucer in England Portugese activity in Africa begins 1415 Gutenberg first prints 1445
1450–1500	Ottoman Turks capture Constantinople, end of Byzantine Empire 1453 Columbus in New World Expulsion of Jews and Moslems from Spain Vasco da Gama sails to India 1498 Massive expansion of world-wide trade
1500–1550	Cesare Borgia nearly becomes pope, 1503 First African slaves brought to New World ca. 1510 Machiavelli: Florentine diplomat and author Protestant Reformation begins Henry VIII breaks with Rome 1534 Copernicus publishes 1543 Council of Trent 1545 begins Counter-Reformation Cortes conquers Aztecs, Pizarro Peru
1550–1600	Reign of Elizabeth I 1558–1603 Galileo and Shakespeare born 1564 Battle of Lepanto stops Turkish expansion, Cyprus falls Spanish Armada
1600–1650	Giordano Bruno burned at stake 1600 Jamestown settled 1607 Telescope invented 1609; Galileo active King James Bible 1611 30 Years War begins 1618 English Civil War begins 1642; Charles I beheaded 1649

Appendix

Temple University's Policy on Academic Dishonesty

Academic Honesty

The students and faculty of Temple University are working together in a common endeavor: to seek the truth, to discover the truth, to speak and to publish the truth. It is an ancient and honorable endeavor, to which teachers and students have dedicated themselves since time immemorial. Out of this long history of dedication to the truth has grown a specific set of requirements governing the ways in which we behave toward one another in the classroom and in which we may use one another's thoughts, words, ideas, and published research. As a Temple student, you will want not only to dedicate yourself generally to the pursuit of truth but also will need to learn the specific rules that govern academic behavior at Temple University.

The most important rules are self-evident and follow inevitably from a respect for the truth. We must not take credit for research, ideas, or words that are not our own. We must not falsify data or results of research. We must not present any work under false pretenses. To be sure that we do not violate these principles, we must learn some specific rules. We must understand exactly what is meant by the three major types of academic dishonesty: plagiarism, violating the rules of an assignment, and cheating on an examination. The faculty of Temple University are confident that if we all understand these few simple rules, we will have no need to worry about academic dishonesty.

Academic Dishonesty

1. Plagiarism

Plagiarism is the unacknowledged use of another person's labor: another person's ideas, words, or assistance.

There are many forms of plagiarism: repeating another person's sentence as your own, adopting a particularly apt phrase as your own, paraphrasing someone else's argument as your own, or even presenting someone else's line of thinking in the development of a thesis as though it were your own. All these forms of plagiarism are prohibited both by the traditional principles of academic honesty and by the regulations of Temple University. Our education and our research encourage us to explore and use the ideas of others, and as writers we will frequently want to use the ideas and even the words of others. It is perfectly acceptable to do so; but we must never submit someone else's work as if it were our own, without giving appropriate credit to the originator. Some sorts of plagiarism are obvious. Students must not copy someone else's examination answer or laboratory report, submit a paper written in whole or in part by someone else, or have a friend do an assignment or take a test for them. Other forms of plagiarism, however, are less obvious. We provide below some guidelines concerning the types of materials that should be acknowledged through an acceptable form of citation.

(a) *Quotations.* Whenever you use a phrase, sentence, or longer passage written (or spoken) by someone else, you must enclose the words in quotation marks and indicate the exact source of the material. This applies also to quotations that you have altered.

(b) *Paraphrasing another's language.* Avoid closely paraphrasing another's words (e.g., substituting an occasional synonym, leaving out or adding an occasional modifier, rearranging the grammar slightly,) just changing the tenses of verbs, and so on. Either quote the material directly, using quotation marks, or put the ideas completely in your own words. In either case, acknowledgment is necessary. Remember: expressing someone else's ideas in your own way does not make them yours.

(c) *Facts.* In a paper, you will often use facts that you have gotten from a lecture, a written work, or some other source. If the facts are well known, it is usually not necessary to provide a source. (In a paper on American history, for example, it would not ordinarily be necessary to give a source for the statement that the Civil War began in 1861 after the inauguration of Abraham Lincoln.) If the facts are not widely known or if the facts were developed or presented by a specific source, however, then you should identify the source for the facts.

(d) *Ideas.* If you use an idea or ideas that you learned from a lecture, written work, or some other source, then you should identify the source. You should identify the source for an idea whether or not you agree with the idea. It does not become your original idea just because you agree with it.

In general, all sources must be identified as clearly, accurately, and thoroughly as possible. When in doubt about whether to identify a source, either cite the source or consult your instructor.

When preparing a paper, you should ask your instructor whether he or she expects you to use footnotes, and whether all sources consulted should appear in a bibliography or only those from which you used material.

2. Violating the Rules of an Assignment

Academic course work is intended to advance the skills, knowledge, and intellectual competence of students. It is important, therefore, that students not behave in such a way as to thwart these intentions. When students are given assignments in a class or laboratory, the instructor will normally explain the rules under which the assignment is to be carried out. A student who does not understand the rules should ask the instructor for clarification. These rules are intended to make the assignment an educational experience and to make certain that the students' accomplishments on the assignment can be fairly evaluated.

Academic cheating is, in general terms, the thwarting or breaking of the general rules of academic work and/or the specific rules of individual courses. It includes falsifying data; submitting, without the instructor's approval, work in one course that was done for another; helping others to plagiarize or cheat from one's own or someone else's work; or actually doing the work of another person.

There are many examples.

If the answers to mathematics problems are in the back of the book, looking them up may produce correct answers, but it will not promote skill, knowledge, or competence. Or if the teacher says that you are not to use a dictionary for a foreign language translation but you use one anyway, you will not have participated in the intended reading exercise. In both of these examples, not only have you cheated yourself of academically useful work but also of any helpful evaluation that the teacher might make. If instructors do not know the kinds of problems that their students are having, they cannot do much to help with those problems.

Another form of academic cheating occurs when work is submitted as if produced according to instructions when actually it is produced by some other means, or is simply invented. When students are given a laboratory assignment, it is assumed that they will carry out the assignment and that their reports will be based on their own laboratory work. A student should not make up data for a report or prepare a report without doing the assignment. If the assignment has called for the collection of data, perhaps through social or laboratory experiment, then the significance of the cheating can be great.

A special case of such cheating occurs when students avoid the expected work of an assignment not by drawing upon the work of others but by drawing upon their own work, already done for another course—for instance, by submitting a paper from one course to fulfill an assignment for another. This is academic cheating, because it frustrates the aims of the assignment. It avoids the development of skill, knowledge, and competence for which the assignment was made. When an instructor assigns a paper to be written outside class, he or she assumes that a student will prepare a paper specifically for that course. This does not mean, of course, that students should avoid building upon their previous work. All education, and especially education within a major field, assumes a continuous building upon what has been previously learned. For the purpose of course work, however, work that you have already done should be regarded as if it were the work of someone else. Specific use of that work must be properly acknowledged, and substitution of that work for a current assignment is a form of cheating, unless specifically permitted by the instructor. If you wish to use a paper that you have prepared for another course, you should obtain permission from your instructor.

3. Cheating on an Examination

Examinations are intended to test your understanding and retention of the material covered in a course.

If you obtain help from other students during the examination, you have cheated. Thus, reading another student's answers while you are taking an examination is cheating.

When an examination is given in class, the instructor will usually assume (or explicitly state) that is a "closed book" examination. If it is, students should not use notes or any other written aids in taking the examination. If you are unsure, ask.

When an examination is given out of class as a "take-home exam," it is normally assumed that you may use class notes, texts, or even material from the library that is properly cited. Your teacher assumes that you will complete the examination alone. You should not obtain help from fellow students in developing your answers and turn them in as if they were your work. Again, if you are unsure, ask.

Penalties for Academic Dishonesty

The penalty for academic dishonesty can vary, from a reprimand and receiving a failing grade for a particular assignment, to failure for the course, to suspension or expulsion from the University. The penalty varies with the nature of the offense, the individual instructor, the department, and the school or college. Some colleges have additional policies, reflecting the unique training that they provide.

Your instructor or dean will provide you with information regarding these additional policies.

Students who believe that they have been unfairly accused may appeal the decision of the instructor, according to the policies and procedures of the school or college. The student should first speak with the instructor. If that does not resolve the matter, the student should speak to the department's ombudsperson or chairperson. If the matter is not satisfactorily resolved at the departmental level, then the student may appeal to the dean or Grievance Committee of the school or college in which the course is given.

A penalty that is beyond the authority of the individual instructor, such as suspension or expulsion, may be imposed by the student's college. Faculty members who believe such a penalty is warranted must make such a recommendation to the student's dean in writing. The student's dean or appropriate college committee will rule on the case and inform the faculty member and student before the end of the following semester.

Students who are dissatisfied with the college's action may appeal the case to the Provost.

PASSED BY THE FACULTY SENATE, April 19, 1989

Notes

The Homeric Hymn to Demeter

1. Persephonê, whom Demeter bore to Zeus. Demeter and Zeus, along with Hades, were among the children of Rhea and Kronos.

2. Another name for Hades.

3. Gaia refers both to the earth and to the Earth Goddess.

4. Hades. Kronos was the second king of the gods.

5. This description is identical to the appearance of Thetis (*Iliad* 24.100) who mourns in advance for the death of Achilles after he has killed Hector.

6. Deô is another name for Demeter. Nine days is a common interval for significant time periods in Homeric epic, especially for periods of transition.

7. Ambrosia and nectar are the food and drink of the Olympian gods.

8. After their defeat of the ruling Titans, the brothers Zeus, Poseidon and Hades divided the universe among themselves, with Zeus receiving the sky, Poseidon the surface and Hades the underworld.

9. There is a gap in the original text here.

10. The word translated as "ramparts"—*krêdemna*—means both "towers of a walled city" and "woman's veil." Thus to sack a city's walls is to tear off the veil from its women. This metaphor allows Homer to foreshadow the inevitable sack of Troy after Hector's death as the epic shows his wife Andromache's veil falling to the ground as she laments her husband. *The Hymn to Demeter* here links the protection of the city with the protection of its female inhabitants.

11. The Greek word here, *kukeôn* denotes the beverage consumed by initiants into the Eleusinian Mysteries.

12. "The yoke of necessity" is a common image in Greek literature; for example, in *The Oresteia* of Aeschylus.

13. Undercutter and Woodcutter are likely names for the worm thought to cause teething.

14. The verb here, *chrieske*, is the same one which, in The New Testament, designates Jesus Christ as *Christos*, "the anointed one."

15. This sequence strongly resembles the failed attempts by the goddess Thetis to immortalize her mortal son Achilles.

16. She is subject to *atê*, blinding delusion, the same rupture of critical judgment experienced by Agamemnon when he agrees to sacrifice his daughter Iphigenia in *Agamemnon* by Aeschylus, and which Agamemnon claims (in Book 19 of *The Iliad*) led him to dishonor Achilles.

17. Oaths are always sworn over the waters of the River Styx, which is in the Underworld.

18. The Kêres.

19. Literally, "most dog-like," possibly an allusion to Sirius, the Dog Star, which was associated with plagues and famine in autumn.

20. A messenger of the gods, the female counterpart to Hermes.

21. The Underworld.

22. Hermes. Argus was a hundred-eyed monster slain by Hermes.

23. An ecstatic female worshipper of the god Dionysos.

24. Rhea was the wife and sister of Kronos, Zeus' father, and thus queen of the generation of Titans, the gods who ruled before the Olympians came to power.

25. The Hymn climaxes with an explanation of the origins of the Eleusinian Mysteries, one of the most important religious cults in Greek antiquity. We know little definite about this cult, just that it has something to do with preparation for an afterlife. It survived well into the Christian era.

Thucydides

1. To be brief, Aristotle recognized a danger in ethical reflection. As he clearly points out, one must be brought up well, and be committed to a life of virtue, if one is to gain a reflective understanding of ethics. At the same time, the ethics of someone not brought up well might actually be undermined by an examination of the centrality of virtue in a good human life. Aristotle, I suggest, was aware of this danger and sought to avoid it by bringing us to the center of his ethical ideas gradually and with some indirection. I have discussed this problem at greater length in a book manuscript entitled, *Politics and Reason.*

Saint Augustine

1. The doctor previously mentioned in Book IV, chapter 3.

2. Ps. 37: 9–11 (38: 8–10).

3. Job 15: 26.

4. Ps. 88: 11 (89: 10).

5. Ps. 84: 6 (85: 5).

6. 1 Pet. 5: 5.

7. John 1: 14.

8. John 1: 1–14.

9. Philipp. 2: 6.

10. Philipp. 2: 7–11.

11. See John 1: 16.

12. Rom. 5: 6.

13. Rom. 8: 32.

14. Matt. 11: 25, 28, 29.

15. Ps. 24: 9 (25: 9).

16. Ps. 24: 18 (25: 18).

17. Matt. 11: 29.

18. Rom. 1: 21–3, 25.
19. Acts 7: 39.
20. Ps. 105: 20 (106: 20).
21. Rom. 9:12.
22. Acts 17: 28.
23. Ps. 29: 11 (30: 10).
24. See Ps. 38: 12 (39: 11).
25. Ex. 3: 14.
26. See Rom. 1: 20.
27. Ps. 72: 28 (73: 28).
28. Wisdom 7: 27.
29. Ps. 15: 2 (16: 2).
30. Gen. 1: 31.
31. Ps. 148: 7–13.
32. Ps. 148: 1–5.
33. Ps. 118: 37 (119: 37).
34. Ecclus. 10: 10.
35. Wisdom 9: 15.
36. Rom. 1: 20.
37. Tim. 2: 5.
38. Rom. 9: 5.
39. John 14: 6.
40. John 1: 14.
41. 1 Cor. 11: 19.
42. Rom. 1: 20.
43. 1 Cor. 8: 1.
44. See 1 Cor. 3: 11; 8: 1.
45. Ps. 2: 11.
46. 1 Cor. 4: 7.
47. Rom. 7: 22.
48. Rom. 7: 23.
49. Dan. 3: 27–32.
50. Ps. 31: 4 (32: 4).
51. John 8: 44.
52. Rom. 7: 24, 25.
53. Prov. 8: 22.
54. See John 14: 30.
55. Col. 2: 14.
56. Ps. 50: 19 (51: 17).
57. Apoc. (Rev.) 21: 2.
58. 11 Cor. 1: 22.
59. Ps. 61: 2, 3 (62: 1, 2).
60. Matt. 11: 25, 28, 29.
61. Ps. 90: 13 (91: 13).
62. 1 Cor. 15: 9.